The Christian Husband's Handbook

The Christian Husband's Handbook

Constantly Pursuing the Treasure You Hold

MARVIN GILBERT
with Amy George

Foreword by Jimmy White

WIPF *&* STOCK · Eugene, Oregon

THE CHRISTIAN HUSBAND'S HANDBOOK
Constantly Pursuing the Treasure You Hold

Copyright © 2020 Marvin Gilbert. All rights reserved. Except for brief quotations in critical publications or reviews, no part of this book may be reproduced in any manner without prior written permission from the publisher. Write: Permissions, Wipf and Stock Publishers, 199 W. 8th Ave., Suite 3, Eugene, OR 97401.

Unless otherwise stated, all Scripture quotations are from the ESV® Bible (The Holy Bible, English Standard Version®), copyright © 2001 by Crossway, a publishing ministry of Good News Publishers. Used by permission. All rights reserved.

Wipf & Stock
An Imprint of Wipf and Stock Publishers
199 W. 8th Ave., Suite 3
Eugene, OR 97401

www.wipfandstock.com

PAPERBACK ISBN: 978-1-5326-9575-9
HARDCOVER ISBN: 978-1-5326-9576-6
EBOOK ISBN: 978-1-5326-9577-3

Manufactured in the U.S.A. 01/14/20

To Treasure-Pursuing Husbands and Future Husbands

"The kingdom of heaven is like treasure hidden in a field, which a man found and covered up. Then in his joy he goes and sells all that he has and buys that field. Again, the kingdom of heaven is like a merchant in search of fine pearls, who, on finding one pearl of great value, went and sold all that he had and bought it."

(MATT 13:44–46)

Contents

Foreword by Jimmy White — ix
Preface — xi
Acknowledgements — xiii
Introduction — xv

1 | Constantly Modeling God's Pursuit — 1
2 | Constantly Applying Biblical Principles — 16
3 | Constantly Pursuing the Moving Target — 33
4 | Constantly Devoted to an Amazing Woman — 50
5 | Constantly Pursuing the Benefits of Marriage — 67
6 | Constantly Pursuing Effective Parenting — 85
7 | Constantly Seducing — 100
8 | Pursuing in Pain — 117
Bibliography — 143

Foreword

No one ever taught me how to be a husband. This vital rite of passage came with no manual, no directions, and no coaching. I was going to be either a good or bad husband based on my observation of my own family. Dr. Marvin Gilbert has addressed a very serious but subtle problem challenging our culture in this present day. In *The Christian Husband's Handbook: Constantly Pursuing the Treasure You Hold*, he examines the core issue of a relentless pursuit of our spouses.

I had the privilege of meeting this author over five years ago when he began serving on the faculty of Southwestern Assemblies of God University in Waxahachie, Texas. We have discussed the role of the Christian husband numerous times. This book is replete with biblical principles that are gleaned from years of ministry. As the Director of Men's Discipleship, I have become increasingly aware that every husband must put into practice biblical principles of pursuing his spouse.

Our culture is confused about marriage and is trying to remove any and all biblical standards related to a husband's healthy pursuit of his spouse. In the midst of this confusion, the Christian husband is challenged to reevaluate the culture's influence on a healthy Christian marriage and to communicate truth.

Gilbert addresses the specific challenge of being a servant leader in the midst of an entitlement mindset. Culture continues to compete for the minds of young men by providing numerous alternatives as valid sources of what the role of a Christian husband should be. Gilbert addresses this reality directly and infers

Foreword

that unless this battle for the biblical principles of a Christian man modeling a holy pursuit of his spouse is won, we will continue to witness a decline of the Christian home that reflects the deterioration of our society in general. He shares candidly what it requires for the Christian husband to model God's pursuit in tangible and visible ways. This book is a must read if this current culture is to realize the true objective of Christian husbanding—living as a servant leader who affirms, honors, and invests in his pursuit of a healthy, biblical marriage.

Dr. Jimmy White
Director of Men's Discipleship
Assemblies of God
Springfield, Missouri

Preface

During my formative years, my father would often make statements that continue to impact my life. For example, he would sometimes tell me that marriage was "a fulltime job." "A full-time job": that bit of wisdom was his only statement that confused me. It confused me because I knew—at least generally—how hard he worked as a longshoreman. He typically left the house before 6:00 am and would not return home again until after 5:00 pm . . . often later. His work on the docks (in Galveston, Texas) certainly seemed like a full-time job to me! So how could this faithful, hard-working man have two full-time jobs? Puzzling!

While in college, I worked summers and Christmas holidays on those same docks, sometimes on the same ship with my father. The work paid great, a blessing for a student, but it was hot, dirty, exhausting, and sometimes dangerous. Typically, I fed 110-pound burlap bags of wheat or rice or whatever into the never-satiated "bellies" of cargo vessels. After 9 to 10 hours of that non-gym workout, all I wanted to do was shower, eat, and crash for the night. This was when, as a longshoreman myself, I began to fully appreciate my father's puzzling marriage maxim.

Dad was just as tired at night as I was, likely more so, but he was still willing to "go for a little walk" with his family on the beach seawall. He happily encouraged my mother to go visit relatives, normally with my siblings and me in tow, even though he would need to "fend for himself" for a week or two at a time. For my father, one full-time job paid good money, the other paid great happiness and peace. Yes, it took me many years to understand

Preface

what he meant, but I never once doubted that his marriage job meant far more to him than his paycheck job.

During my first two decades, I observed my father constantly pursue my mother (and us children) on a daily basis. I could never have phrased it that way as a child; I did not have the words then. I think I do now. This book is my attempt to describe a married man's second "full-time" job: the constant pursuit of the woman he loves. My hope is that its message is clear, compelling, and—at least for some readers—life changing.

Acknowledgements

I wish to acknowledge my wife, Rosie, for the enormous contribution she made to this work. For more than forty-seven years, she has been my friend, ministry colleague, and sounding board for my strange ideas. For the last year, she has been my diligent and skilled copy editor: for *Sweaty, Sore, Sometimes Hungry* (© 2019: Resource Publications) and now for *The Handbook*. She does not particularly enjoy editing, yet she has done this . . . and done it well . . . out of love for me, love for Jesus, and belief that the words on a well-edited page might change readers for the better. Thank you, Rosie! I am deeply grateful for your labor of love.

I also wish to acknowledge the rich contribution Amy George made to this book. Her "Listen to the Lady" reflections have enlivened this book, contributing a "flavor" to the instructional "soup" that I could not. Thank you, Amy, for "spicing up" the final product as you have done.

Finally, I acknowledge the encouragement of Drs. Amy and Danny Alexander. In particular, Amy's affirmation that my "voice" comes through clearly in my written work continues to inspire me to get the words right—to search out and eliminate as much voice-distorting "static" as possible. Thank you, both, for believing!

Introduction

The eight chapters composing *The Christian Husband's Handbook* offer hope and guidance to men desiring to live "happily ever after." Some men may view this ever-after goal as distant, perhaps even unreachable, especially as the wedding anniversaries role past. Marriage, like most relationships in life, has a way of settling into a predictable pattern. For some, that pattern could be summarized as "boringly ever after" or even "sadly ever after."

I am optimist enough to believe that the majority of Christian men are, most of the time, enjoying the life they continue to create with their wives under Christ's lordship. The research literature supports this optimistic conclusion, as demonstrated throughout the book. Still, most men know that questions about marriage surface from time to time:

- Could my marriage be better, stronger?
- What should masculine leadership in my home look like in this hypersensitive age, when sexism, misogyny, and "toxic masculinity" are derided in the media and social networks?
- Is lasting change really possible after __ years of marriage?

This book, as a whole, seeks to empower men to answer these and other questions about marriage. Broad in scope, *The Handbook* is designed for men who are living out a variety of "ever after" scenarios.

Introduction

Many books on the topic of Christian marriage are intended for female readers or, at best, for couples. The eight chapters in *The Handbook* are written exclusively to and for men; each chapter is designed to inspire and empower them to be the best husbands they can be.

The first two chapters lay a biblical foundation for Christian marriage: they place the responsibility for a thriving, growing marriage squarely on the husband. His relentless pursuit of the woman he has already won reflects, even if poorly, God's relentless pursuit of both husband and wife.

1. "Constantly Modeling God's Pursuit": The Holy Spirit exemplifies a husband's continuous pursuit of the woman he loves. That pursuit is always gentle, never threatening, and always intended to bless.

2. "Constantly Applying Biblical Principles": The marriage principles of loving, serving, honoring, and collaborating are firmly grounded in God's Word and are clearly applicable to a thriving marriage. Collaboration, in particular, characterizes a home filled with happiness and mutual esteem.

Chapters three, four, and five detail the objectives and methods of a man's constant pursuit.

3. "Constantly Pursuing the Moving Target": Husbands and wives are in constant motion, changing as both individuals and as spouses. This always-in-motion reality challenges a Christian husband to stay flexible and to pursue creatively his ever-changing wife.

4. "Constantly Devoted to an Amazing Woman": A loving husband will honor the growth taking place in his wife, modeling dynamic growth himself. In the process, he will eagerly remain devoted to his wife's multidimensional pleasure.

5. "Constantly Pursuing the Benefits of Marriage": Marriage can enrich a man's life in *so many* ways, from living longer to living better (financially, physically, and emotionally). The

Introduction

joy of living with a sensuous, charming woman is another powerful benefit of marriage.

The three remaining chapters address family-relevant and marriage-specific situations.

6. "Constantly Pursuing Effective Parenting": This chapter highlights the skills of Christian *fathering*, just as the other seven chapters highlight Christian *husbanding*. This chapter defines the ultimate goal of parenting: launching relationally competent offspring into the world, fully equipped to find their place as adults who value themselves, others, and marriage.
7. "Constantly Seducing": Chapter seven focuses on the intimate life of husband and wife, emphasizing the various avenues of seduction available to a Christian husband. Of special interest, the section titled "Exclusiveness Is Seductive" admonishes a husband to comprehensively forsake "all others" for the joy of constantly seducing his wife as a one-woman man.
8. "Pursuing in Pain": The final chapter offers pursuit strategies for difficult marital situations, when pursuing hurts. A Christian man is not immune to those less-than-ideal circumstances that threaten his marriage. When hurting, his responsibility to pursue his wife remains undiminished; pain cannot justify seeking a quick way out. In the worst-case scenario of divorce, a God-fearing man remains responsible to pursue peace with the significant people in his life—including his former wife.

Two unique features of this book merit specific introductions. The first is a section titled "Listen to the Lady" included near the end of each chapter. In these short reflection pieces, Mrs. Amy George enriches and illustrates one or more key topics. Her contributions uniquely impact the reader. A wise Christian husband will attend closely to what she says; her "voice" likely sounds much like the voice of many Christian wives.

The second unique feature, "Deal with It," directs the reader to valuable resources for enriching each chapter's content. These

Introduction

"Deal with It" sections provide suggestions for additional reading, reflection questions, prayer guides, and action steps:

- Read and View
- Think it Through
- Pray it Through
- Act on It

The first three "Deal with It" sections are suitable for group study, discussion, and accountability. The "Act on It" section is designed to empower growth-facilitating discussions with the reader's wife.

My hope is that this handbook will become a comprehensive source of hope, growth, and change. May each marriage impacted by its content thrive, with God's rich blessing upon it.

1

Constantly Modeling God's Pursuit

"those strong Feet that followed, followed after. . . . with unhurrying chase,
And unperturbèd pace, Deliberate speed, majestic instancy,
They beat."

FRANCIS THOMPSON[1]

INTRODUCTION

It is paradoxical. Pursuing something you already hold may initially appear illogical. Typically, we pursue things (or people) not yet in our grasp. An essential academic degree, a dream job, a particular status in life, a trophy buck in November: either you have it or you don't. That logic is clear and compelling.

Occasionally, though, we encounter situations that defy this clear-cut logic. Take physical fitness as an example. You can work hard to get in the best condition you have been in decades. The bathroom scales say you have it. Your waistline says you have it.

1. Taken from http://www.blueridgejournal.com/poems/ft-hound.htm.

Your close friends tell you how good you look. Do you stop working out hard because you "have it?" No! You *continue to pursue* what you already have: great health and physical fitness. You know that if you stop the pursuit, you will lose what you have gained . . . what you already hold. Yes, the pursuit of fitness is paradoxical; it also serves as a useful metaphor for a magnificent marriage.

In this chapter[2] I argue that you must constantly pursue what you already have. As a Christian husband, you already have a wife. She said "Yes" to your marriage proposal, perhaps decades ago. Given this, you may have become (or will become) tempted to relax the effort or even to stop pursuing her altogether. This book invites you to resist this temptation. Fight it, sir! Your *constant pursuit* of what you already hold dear will enrich your marriage and bless your wife and children. Pursue her:

- just as the Holy Spirit gently continues to pursue you,
- for *her* welfare, even though you will benefit enormously from the effort,
- without stalking or smothering,
- to hear her respond (eagerly, passionately) with "Yes" to your rest-of-your-life proposals.

RELENTLESS PURSUIT: "THE HOUND OF HEAVEN"

English poet Francis Thompson, while recovering from addiction to the morphine-derivative laudanum, depicted in haunting, stirring verse God's constant pursuit of his lost and self-destructive child. This epic poem begins:

> I FLED Him, down the nights and down the days;
> I fled Him, down the arches of the years;
> I fled Him, down the labyrinthine ways
> Of my own mind; and in the mist of tears

---

2. Actually, I based the entire book on this argument.

Constantly Modeling God's Pursuit

I hid from Him, and under running laughter.
Up vistaed slopes I sped;
And shot, precipitated,
Adown Titanic glooms of chasmèd fears,
From those strong Feet that followed, followed after.
But with unhurrying chase,
And unperturbèd pace,
Deliberate speed, majestic instancy,
They beat—and a Voice beat
More instant than the Feet—
'All things betray thee, who betrayest Me.'[3]

This lengthy work, published in 1893, depicts in stunning clarity the poet's desperate flight from God's relentless pursuit.[4] God patiently explained, stanza by stanza, that worldly pleasures always enticed the poet, pulling him in the wrong direction. What God desired to take from this fear-driven wanderer was not intended to punish him. Rather, the Hound of Heaven pursued only to help him find the path of life. The happiness he thought he would lose, God instructed, would not be lost at all; it was "stored for thee at home." So, "rise, clasp My hand, and come!"

The poet then wonders if the gloom he has felt was just the shade created by the hand of God reaching out to him. The happiness he sought by running away, perhaps modeled on the prophet Jonah's flight from God, had been constantly pursuing him.

RELENTLESS PURSUIT: KEY BIBLICAL STATEMENTS

A Christian husband must understand that his unending pursuit of his wife must be modeled on God's relentless pursuit of those created in his image. That pursuit is love-based, is depicted in

---

3. A stirring adaptation of this poem is available at "The Hound of Heaven: A Modern Adaptation."
4. Analysis of the poem is based on Cummings, "The Hound of Heaven."

some of Christ's most profound parables, and reflects the very nature of God.

Who Loved First?

The Christian faith is, in essence, reactionary: we love because God *first* loved us (1 John 4:19). We surrender to Christ because he surrendered to the Father's will. Even if we become known to others as God chasers,[5] he remains the Originator of the chase! Our purest, most-focused pursuit of God is ultimately a response to his relentless pursuit of us. Only three chapters into the Old Testament, God came pursuing our first parents, asking, *"Where are you?"* (Gen 3:9),[6] as they vainly tried to hide their sin and shame from him. He was then, and unchangeably remains, the Great Pursuer! In Ezekiel 34:11, God promised, *"Behold, I, I myself will search for my sheep and will seek them out."* Jesus may have reflected on this verse when confronting the crowd seeking more miracle bread (John 6:26). He boldly explained the practical implication of God's search: *"no one can come to me unless the Father who sent me draws him"* (John 6:44; see also verses 37 and 45).

Two chapters earlier, Jesus had revealed the Father's pursuing heart to a most unlikely audience of one: *"the hour is coming, and is now here, when the true worshipers will worship the Father in spirit and truth, for the Father is seeking such people to worship him"* (John 4:23). How stunning this unexpected message of hope must have been for that morally broken Samaritan woman at Jacob's well! Deeply impacted by his pursuit, she managed to convince her entire village to *"come, see a man"* who had pursued her and won her sin-damaged heart (4:29).

---

5. See Tenney, *The God Chasers.*

6. All Scripture quotations, unless otherwise stated, are from the English Standard Version.

Parables of Pursuit

Three gripping parables in Luke 15 brilliantly illustrate God's relentless pursuit of the lost, and his great joy resulting from finding them. The parable of the *lost sheep* vividly pictures God's pursuit of his wayward people[7] (aka, "sheep"):

> *What man of you, having a hundred sheep, if he has lost one of them, does not leave the ninety-nine in the open country, and go after the one that is lost, until he finds it? And when he has found it, he lays it on his shoulders, rejoicing. And when he comes home, he calls together his friends and his neighbors, saying to them, "Rejoice with me, for I have found my sheep that was lost."* (15:4-6)

In the parable of the *lost coin* (15:8-9), a desperate woman frantically searches for what she had lost. She sweeps her entire house, looking high and low for that one coin:

> *And when she has found it, she calls together her friends and neighbors, saying, "Rejoice with me, for I have found the coin that I had lost."* (15:9)

Her intensely focused search for that coin beautifully depicts the Father's seeking-pursuing heart.

Finally, the grieving father in the parable of the prodigal *lost son* constantly scanned the road to his house for his rebellious, wandering son. Then, on that special day, while the young man *"was still a long way off, his father saw him and felt compassion, and ran and embraced him and kissed him"* (15:20).

The Relentless Trinity

Like his Father who sent him, Jesus was a relentless Pursuer. In Matthew 4 (verses 18-22), he called his first disciples, using his unique *"Follow me"* invitation-challenge. Luke 19 depicts his pursuit of a small lost man, Zacchaeus. Jesus invited himself (and his

---

7. This was the very pursuit God had earlier promised Israel in Ezekiel 34 after rebuking the nation's spiritual rulers.

hungry followers) to lunch and into that greedy man's heart! During their sinner-transforming meal, Jesus revealed his life's mission: *"Today salvation has come to this house, since he also is a son of Abraham. For the Son of Man came to seek and to save the lost"* (19:9–10). Like Father, like Son! In fact, all three members of the Trinity relentlessly seek the lost.

The Holy Spirit's active involvement in salvation, as promised by Jesus, is clearly described in John 16:8–9. God initiates this lifegiving relationship, then rejoices greatly when the lost are found: when rebels repent, when sinners surrender. The Bible is, in fact, one giant lost-and-found love story! Without doubt, God can teach Christian husbands a great deal about pursuit—not of sinful Samaritan women, but of their beloved, cherished wives.

RELENTLESS BEFORE-AND-AFTER PURSUIT: LESSONS FROM THE HOLY SPIRIT

The Holy Spirit relentlessly pursues both sinners and saints, restless until God's children resemble, with ever-increasing clarity, Christ Jesus their Lord. A Christian husband, when at his best, models his interaction with his wife on that divine pursuit.

He Pursues Sinners

The Holy Spirit convicts sinners of their sins! Conviction is one of his specialties as the active Expression of God's will, for God neither wills nor desires *"that any should perish, but that all should reach repentance"* (2 Pet 3:9). His conviction intensifies and magnifies the sinfulness of sin and the accompanying sense of lostness we experience apart from God. Like the poet running from the Hound, some sinners resent the Spirit's intervention, angry they are no longer at ease in their sin. They fear the loss of their illusionary freedom, independence, and control. Happily, many other

Constantly Modeling God's Pursuit

sinners yield to the Spirit's relentless pursuit, turning in repentance and faith in Christ to receive salvation.[8]

He Pursues Saints

Salvation is critically important. It is, however, only the beginning point of the Spirit's work in our lives. He comforts and corrects, instructs and purifies, empowers and reveals the glories of our resurrected Lord. Most of all, the Holy Spirit works *on* us and *through* us to perfect and sanctify us (literally, to *set us apart*) to Christ. Peter included *"the sanctifying work of the Spirit"* as part of the Trinity's empowerment for Christian living (1 Pet 1:2, NIV). Paul echoed the same thought in 2 Thessalonians 2:13: *"But we ought always to give thanks to God for you, brothers beloved by the Lord, because God chose you as the firstfruits to be saved, through sanctification by the Spirit and belief in the truth."*[9]

A detailed study of the Spirit's work prior to, during, and after salvation lies well beyond the scope of this handbook; excellent resources abound on this topic.[10] His transforming work does, however, illustrate beautifully how husbands should, with gentleness and respect, pursue their wives.

A Bride's Immediate Transformation

Salvation is a life-altering spiritual moment for every Christian. Similarly, a wedding is a life-altering legal and relational event. In a traditional[11] Christian marriage, a woman changes her last name, social identity, and primary allegiance.[12] She publicly con-

   8. Read John 6:44.
   9. See also 1 Thess 5:23 for another perspective on sanctification.
   10. For example, Allen and Swain, *Sanctification*, and Powlison, *How Does Sanctification Work?*
   11. This is true in many cultures, especially in the West.
   12. As expressed by the traditional phrase, "Who gives this woman to be wed to this man?" See also the section titled "Exclusiveness Is Seductive" in chapter 7.

fesses her love for "this man" and willingly binds herself to him in a Christ-exalting, one-flesh covenant. This radical transformation of two people at marriage dimly reflects the far more astounding transformation of the lost through salvation.

A wife's marriage transformation is preceded by hundreds, perhaps thousands, of hours of consistent pursuit: her husband's pre-wedding patient, loving, unswerving pursuit of his beloved. Just as the Spirit pursues those deeply loved by the Father, so a man pursues his future wife. He seeks to win her heart, seeks to hear her say "Yes" to his proposal and, later, "I will" during their wedding ceremony.

A Groom's Continuing Pursuit

The application of this comparison must be obvious. As the Spirit continues to pursue believers for their sanctification, so a Christian husband must continue his pursuit after the wedding. The new Mrs. Right continues to need her new husband's gentle, comforting, and consistent pursuit. His influence in her life, in a real sense, begins only after the wedding. The Holy Spirit constantly comforts believers, assuring them they are blessed by God's grace *"in the Beloved"* (Eph 1:6). In similar manner, a Christian husband should consistently assure his wife that she is fully accepted in his heart: safe, loved, respected, admired, and desired. His influence will, over the years, profoundly impact her, motivating her to either respond to him with an open, trusting heart, or retreat with a closed, wounded heart.[13]

How long should a husband pursue his wife? And what about his needs? Should she ever pursue him? Each couple must work out the dynamics of pursuit in their marriage: those dynamics will likely shift some as they grow together. I argue throughout this book that the husband must be the primary pursuer in a Christian marriage, even though he may occasionally enjoy being pursued! Ultimately, he is free to stop pursuing his wife when the Spirit stops pursuing him—and that is *never!*

---

13. See the section titled "Pursuing a Wounded Heart" in chapter 8.

Constantly Modeling God's Pursuit

RELENTLESS PURSUIT: NEITHER STALKING NOR SMOTHERING

The Holy Spirit pursues us for *our* benefit; God is complete in himself, needing nothing from us. Yet he longs to see his children thriving holistically and knows this is possible *only* in his presence. The challenge to emulate the Spirit's loving, for-our-benefit pursuit is clear: a Christian husband must selflessly seek *her* good. And her good sometimes requires occasional (hopefully brief) withdrawal to give her space to grow and opportunity to process life. The Holy Spirit constantly hovers near those he loves; a husband, no matter how loving, cannot.

Stalking sometimes begins as a distorted expression of concern and desire to help. Unfortunately, it can easily begin to dominate a marriage relationship, fueled by a husband's[14] distrust and fear. This perversion of gentle pursuit benefits only the stalker, never the "object" (victim) of his alleged affection. Manipulation and over-control are *never* honest, loving, selfless, or Christ-like. Fear-driven actions threaten, not bless, the stalkee. Thus, Christian husbands must constantly pursue their wives without cajoling, stalking, smothering, or manipulating them. The ultimate Model for this unceasing pursuit is called the *Comforter*, not the Controller. He is our *Advocate*, not our Accuser; the role of accuser belongs to another (Rev 12:10). Husbands must get this perspective right or nothing they do when proactively loving their wives will be welcomed or life-enhancing.

REJECTING A PURSUIT-AND-CONQUEST MENTALITY

This section identifies unique challenges men face concerning the nature of their lifetime pursuit. The payoff for pursuit is not a trophy on a wall, but a thriving-in-marriage woman who continues to grow in love with her husband. Conquest has nothing to do with *that* payoff.

---

14. In a marriage characterized by stalking, the husband is typically the stalker.

Managing the Challenge of Conquest

I end my contribution to this chapter with several words of discomfort for us men in general. Most of us are conquest-driven: biologically wired and culturally trained to win . . . or at least *try* to win. Some men actively seek new challenges on a regular basis; routine for them is painful. If their employment does not provide adequate stimulation, they engage in pastimes that *resemble* work! Others, paradoxically, both seek out and hate new tests. Yet they tend to keep signing up for more. Our urge to win, to defeat, to overcome impacts us deeply . . . from fighting wars to passing the guy who just cut us off on the freeway, from planning corporate takeovers to taking a trophy animal with one shot.

Our attraction to testing situations implies we have an enemy to defeat, an obstacle to surmount, or a personal limitation to overcome. If we succeed, sometimes with the "deck" stacked against us, we feel victorious and affirmed as human beings. If we fail, well . . . at least we gave it our best! And we will come back stronger than ever next time.

This intense desire to succeed against all odds in new challenges is totally appropriate in some arenas. It is, however, a guaranteed *relationship-killer* in the courtship and marriage arenas. Without doubt, a new relationship with a potential mate is thrilling. Adrenaline is pumping, pulse is racing, senses are keenly focused. You focus all of your time, money, and effort on her. Like a hunter in the field, you spot her, trail her,[15] bathe often to keep your scent down, and attempt to win her heart. And then . . .

Rejecting the Trophy-Taking Mentality

Unfortunately, some men have *no clue* what to do next—after winning the women they desire. Their uncertainty is quite common, especially if they were raised without an effective Christian role model.[16] They find that their hard-earned trophy, the woman's

---

15. But *without* stalking her!
16. See the section titled "Pursuing 'Uphill'" in chapter 8.

heart, suddenly becomes a burden rather than a treasured source of joy. Intensifying this dilemma, some men are *so* good at pursuit they become addicted to its adrenaline rush. One "victory" leads to another, then another, and another! How many hearts are enough? When does this new-trophy pursuit end?

Sir, she is *not* an object to be "taken and mounted"[17] in the "trophy room" of your mind or your bed. She is a woman created in the image of God: beautiful, sensitive, and—her strengths and gifts notwithstanding—relatively fragile. Her heart is especially prone to cracks and chips; it can be totally broken by a persistent trophy hunter. That heart breaker may himself have been deceived by pathetic role models,[18] believing that the thrill is in the chase, not in the adventure of a lifetime thereafter. Still, he remains morally responsible for the heart damage he inflicts through this pursue-and-conquest approach to romantic relationships. Prior to his departure from home for college, I advised my son, "Never try to win a woman's heart unless you are willing to take care of it once you have it."[19] (That advice still stands: feel free to share it with your son!)

Men addicted to collecting heart trophies are not legal hunters, just worthless poachers! Illegal and dangerous, some continue these pursuit-and-conquest relationships even after they marry. Broken hearts, families, careers, and dreams all contribute to the growing collateral damage inflicted by these ego-driven, adrenalin-addicted poachers. The scandals that began emerging in the power-saturated arenas of politics and entertainment in 2006, eventually birthing the #metoo movement,[20] graphically illustrate this sad reality!

---

17. Pun intended.
18. Again, see "Pursuing 'Uphill'" in chapter 8.
19. This statement was part of the unpublished collected wisdom I presented to my son, Stephen, just before he left home (in Kenya) to start his college career (in the USA).
20. See https://metoomvmt.org/.

Aiming Higher than One "Yes"

A pursuit-and-conquest mentality can never serve as an unshakable foundation for a Christ-exalting marriage. As noted earlier, a new relationship generates thrilling emotions. Consider a hypothetical couple: George and Sandy. They have just begun a serious courtship. With his thoughts constantly on Sandy, George may find himself walking into closed doors (as I did when I first met my wife, Rosie). He may lose sleep, appetite, and focus because of Sandy. George should enjoy that amazing season of growing wonder and discovery! Deeply satisfying marriages, however, are based on for-the-long-haul commitments, not adrenaline rushes.

If the thrill ends for George when Sandy finally (ultimately) says "Yes," he has set his "sights" *far* too low. He must "aim" much higher than hearing only one "Yes." The true test of successful pursuit, in my opinion, consists of hearing her passionate, open-hearted "Yes" whispered 18,250 times (or more) as a won-again-and-again woman! Phrased differently, George should "aim" to hear Sandy respond to his tender pursuit for 50 years (or more) in their almost-never-boring marriage. (Do the math!)

To the point, sir: if all you want is a thrilling conquest and an ego-boosting trophy, go hunt an elk in Colorado. Leave women alone.

LISTEN TO THE LADY:[21]
ARCHAEOLOGIST OVER TREASURE HUNTER

My husband Calvin is a true movie buff. He has spent many hours in theaters and has a remarkable capacity for remembering details of movies he has viewed. We have watched some movies more than once, including those in the *Indiana Jones* franchise. The original trilogy gives one a clear sense of the title character; Jones goes on risky journeys to attain rare treasures. His formula for success is not dependent on merely attaining something precious for

---

21. The "Listen to the Lady" section appears at the end of each chapter. Professor Amy George is the lady who contributed a married woman's perspective on selected major topics in the book.

Constantly Modeling God's Pursuit

the thrill of it, but on preserving its value. Like his boss, a museum curator, Jones "treasures" each new find. He is both an archaeologist and a professor of archaeology, which means he is a serious student of his field.

For a wife to feel gently pursued, her husband must be a serious student of her needs. Discovering what is important to her . . . desiring to learn her thoughts, values, and personal aspirations . . . require him to listen carefully to her. He must value her *far* beyond attaining her affections just long enough to put a ring on her finger.

Proverbs 31:10 describes the priceless value of a virtuous woman: *"An excellent wife who can find? She is far more precious than jewels."* Jewels are never tossed aside haphazardly. They are polished, protected, and valued for their unique inherent worth. When precious gems discovered, their care becomes someone's priority.

I once had the opportunity to see the Hope Diamond at the Smithsonian National Museum of Natural History in Washington, DC. The tour guide gave a detailed explanation about the layers of security surrounding this deep blue diamond, one of the rarest varieties in the world. Clearly the curators at the Smithsonian didn't just shove the stone into a generic display case. Instead, the very temperature and humidity of the gem's high-tech container are monitored continuously. Even testing this priceless jewel demands extreme precautions to preserve its integrity.[22]

We care best for what we value most. Like both Indiana Jones and the Smithsonian curators, husbands must attentively care for their wives. A man's gentle pursuit of his wife is shown through his care: the words he uses toward her and the time and attention he affords her. He would do well to remember her value in her Father's eyes.

(As a side note, I once had an archaeology professor who joked with his wife that as she got older, he'd still be in love with her because he was interested in old things. I'm not sure how many "brownie points" that statement initially got him, but I do know they've been married for many decades, so at least she has a sense of humor.)

22. See Caputo, "Testing the Hope Diamond."

DEAL WITH IT

Read and View

1. Bingham, "What Is Sanctification?"[23]
2. Fonseca, "25 Important Bible Verses About Conviction."[24]
3. Desroches, "Holy Spirit: Conviction of Sin."[25]

Think It Through

1. Is the Holy Spirit ("the Hound of Heaven") still pursuing you? What evidence do you see of his pursuit?
2. Is the challenge to constantly pursue their wives unfair to men? Justify your answer.
3. How has your pursuit of your wife changed since you first met her?
4. What specific changes or transformations did your wife face when she married you?

Pray It Through

1. Confess any "heart damage" sins you inflicted during your past pursuit-and-conquest behaviors. (Give thanks, instead, if you have never chipped, cracked, or broken a woman's heart.)
2. Embrace and welcome again (or for the first time) the abiding presence of the Hound of Heaven in your life.
3. Pray for wisdom to distinguish between gentle, comforting pursuit and stalking-smothering behaviors as you relate to your wife. (Repent for the latter behaviors, if you recall times of stalking or smothering her.)

---

23. https://www.ligonier.org/blog/what-sanctification/.
24. https://biblereasons.com/conviction/.
25. YouTube video: https://youtu.be/7njd19ya6eg.

Constantly Modeling God's Pursuit

ACT ON IT

1. View with your wife: "The Hound of Heaven: A Modern Adaptation."[26]

    - Discuss with her your primary "take aways" from this video.

    - Discuss with your wife the concept of trophy hunting as used in this chapter. Was she a "trophy" to you while dating? Explain your answer to her.

2. Explain to your wife how this chapter has impacted you.

---

26. YouTube video: https://youtu.be/RXlgz4aBKt8.

2

Constantly Applying Biblical Principles

"Apply yourself wholly to the Scriptures, and apply the Scriptures wholly to yourself."

JOHANN A. BENGEL[1]

INTRODUCTION

The contrast between culture and Scripture could not be sharper! Society now promotes, or at least tacitly approves, a pathetic view of marriage. This once-exalted social institution is now consistently characterized by either decades of passionless mediocrity or vow-destroying sexual flings (and eventual destruction). Movie and television plots thrive on marital unfaithfulness and selfishly shattered covenants. Young adults, if they marry at all,[2] often enter marriage pessimistic about its future. Many of their age mates (and *their* parents, too) have "crashed and burned" in highly

1. Taken from https://www.christianquotes.info/.

2. See Fry, "More Americans Are Living without Partners," for the shocking research data generated by the Pew Research Center.

destructive relationships. Such pessimism is, unfortunately, often grounded in reality.

Our culture seems to reluctantly tolerate marriage initiated in the name of "love," especially if the far-too-expensive wedding is "beautiful." Often, however, a given couple's professed love consists of little more than hormone-driven attraction and self-serving motives. The notion of a three-person sacramental covenant between bride, groom, and God is never even mentioned in many wedding ceremonies.

Christian couples have no special immunity to devastating divorces. They do have, however, access to a powerful, biblical foundation capable of informing, guiding, and—when needed—confronting them. That foundation includes the four pillars ("principles") explored in this chapter:

- the loving principle,
- the serving principle,
- the honoring principle,
- the collaborating principle.

When fitted together skillfully and patiently, these principles allow couples to build thriving, growing, for-the-long-haul marriages. Only principle-grounded marriages can withstand the relational storms that ravage foundationless marriages (see Matt 7:24–27).

THE LOVING PRINCIPLE

"Husbands, love your wives, as Christ loved the church and gave himself up for her. . . . In the same way husbands should love their wives as their own bodies. He who loves his wife loves himself."
(Eph 5:25, 28)

The New Testament sets the standard for husbanding high; mediocre efforts will not do! The ultimate Role Model for wife loving is Jesus Christ. Sadly, some Christian husbands are content to settle for a more "realistic" model. After all, who can love exactly like Jesus, with his unwavering persistence, patience, perseverance, and other admirable words beginning with the letter *p*? No one can! What was Paul thinking when he wrote these sentences? Did he write simply to frustrate and discourage the husbands reading his apostolic love letter? Was he issuing an impossible-to-obey command?

Rejecting the WIIFM Style of Loving

Take courage, sir! The "loving principle" expressed in Ephesians 5 addresses the *style*, not absolute quantity and quality, of love. Paul essentially challenged husbands to embrace the *Christ* style of loving: to emulate the Savior's tender, sacrificial love for the church he came to make glorious. Christ-style love, detailed below, focuses on what I have to *give*, not on what I want to *get*. A *what's-in-it-for-me* (WIIFM)[3] approach to marital commitment forms the antithesis of Christ-style husbanding. In fact, WIIFM characterizes most commitments made in this sin-damaged world. No matter how well packaged or logically justified, WIIFM *always* motivates and justifies getting, not giving. This self-centered style of husbanding drains, never replenishes, a marital relationship. Christian marriages die by the thousands each year because WIIFM-oriented husbands fail to emulate the Christ style.

Embracing the Christ Style of Loving

The Christ style of loving is characterized by personal *sacrifice*, not personal *satisfaction*. Never passive, this active-loving style of relating is most easily discerned in loving deeds (though loving words also reflect the Christ style). A husband emulating the Christ style proactively initiates connection with his wife, even when he feels hurt or offended. In short, he leads in the marital "dance." Without question, a wife is the heart of any family, but a Christian husband is its guide and pace setter.

---

3. See the Introduction to chapter 5 for elaboration on the WIIFM question.

Constantly Applying Biblical Principles

Christ-style loving propels me to eagerly pursue my wife's highest good. It motivates me to focus on her, not me: on her needs, not mine.[4] Yet this style of loving is not totally altruistic. Yes, Paul set the standard high for husbands. He then observed, in so many words, that if a husband prioritizes his wife's highest good, *really* good things happen to him, too! My willingness to sacrificially embrace the Christ style of marital love ultimately provides a huge payoff for me. If I love my wife as Christ loved the church, she will be extraordinarily happy . . . and eager to meet my needs in return.[5] Yes, this approach is risky, but the payoff is much higher than *any* outcome I could manipulate using a WIIFM strategy. To be honest, my risks are small compared to hers when she finally told God, the preacher, and me "I do."[6]

Herein lies one of the great paradoxes of the Christian faith: selfless love is ultimately self-serving! I confess openly that I love my body. The smartest thing I can do, then, is love my wife selflessly. The implication in Paul's argument is clear: my secure, happy wife will take excellent care of me (including my body) if I love her as Christ loves his church.

THE SERVING PRINCIPLE

"The Son of Man came not to be served but to serve." (Mark 10:45)

Loving as Jesus loved, serving as Jesus served, these selfless acts form the antithesis of personal entitlement. Jesus loved his own as a servant leader, willing to kneel before his disciples to teach them as their servant. A Christian husband, seeking to love as Jesus loves, serves his wife and children sacrificially.

---

4. In *Sacred Marriage*, author Gary Thomas proposes that the purpose of marriage is to make spouses *holy*, not necessarily happy! God can use even dysfunctional marriages to work his will out in believers. *Sacred Marriage* is an excellent motivational check for Christian husbands.

5. Again, see the Introduction to chapter 5.

6. Review the section titled "Relentless Before-and-After Pursuit: Lessons from the Holy Spirit" in chapter 1. See also the section titled "Exclusiveness Is Seductive" in chapter 7.

Rejecting an Entitlement Worldview

"At your service!" This now archaic phrase is rarely heard or used today, definitely not so in marriage. Popular culture embraces the exact opposite view; the incessant promotion of personal entitlement is unrelenting. An entitlement mentality motivates and justifies the WIIFM worldview. Responsibility-rejecting entitlement is now *so* pervasive in, and so destructive to, society that even secular mental health workers have begun openly expressing concern. Some of them now see entitlement as a pathological issue that must be addressed urgently.[7]

Entitlement weakens the fabric of any culture because it negates any sense of civic duty or responsibility. The stirring inauguration speech of President John Kennedy[8] still inspires true patriots: "Ask not what your country can do for you—ask what you can do for your country." In our increasingly entitlement-oriented culture, relatively few muster the moral courage to answer the Kennedy-motivated question: What can I give back?

Applying the entitlement mentality to marriage, WIIFM-perverted husbands believe they are entitled to their wives' labor and bodies: both on demand! And they freely use their superior strength and aggressive nature to enforce that demeaning view of women. This you-exist-to-serve-me (YETSM) philosophy of marriage is normative for men who have never seen a *real* man kneel to serve his wife and children. Unfortunately, this Christ-denying YETSM philosophy infects many Christian marriages, resulting in power-based leadership in the home.

Ugly is ugly, even when covered with a paper-thin veneer of misinterpreted Scripture. YETSM-oriented husbands often cite 1 Corinthians 11:3[9] to justify their selfish, ego-driven domination of

---

7. Boyes, "9 Types of Entitlement Tendencies." See also Truitt, "Beware of the Entitlement Mentality."

8. Delivered January 21, 1961. See Kennedy, "Ask Not."

9. *"But I want you to understand that the head of every man is Christ, the head of a wife is her husband, and the head of Christ is God."*

their wives. Such men understand *nothing* about God nor the true nature of Christ-emulating leadership.

Embracing a Servant-Leadership Worldview

Jesus told his disciples they were correct to call him *"Teacher and Lord"* (John 13:13). As their Lord, Jesus was the only One entitled to be served by them. Yet he abandoned his justifiable entitlement in order to teach them a profound lesson about life in his upside-down Kingdom. Wrapped in a servant's towel, he knelt to wash twenty-four dirty feet (John 13:4–5), including two that would soon carry their owner into utter darkness and betrayal (13:30).

Willingly serving another person from a position of strength and integrity empowers both the server *and* the servee. Servant leaders in the corporate world choose to embrace the upside-down model of organizational functioning that Jesus first illustrated in John 13. Robert Greenleaf discovered that servant leadership[10] often differentiates companies that thrive and those that struggle or even self-destruct. Greenleaf's insights into true leadership greatness continue to impact the business world. A recent Amazon book search for "servant leadership" returned 1,078 titles of interest!

Greenleaf urged corporate leaders to focus on

> the growth and wellbeing of people and the communities to which they belong. While traditional leadership generally involves the accumulation and exercise of power by one at the "top of the pyramid," servant leadership is different. The servant-leader shares power, puts the needs of others first and helps people develop and perform as highly as possible.[11]

---

10. "What Is Servant Leadership?"

11. "What Is Servant Leadership?" The Robert K. Greenleaf Center for Servant Leadership exists "to advance the awareness, understanding and practice of servant leadership by individuals and organizations." See details at https://www.greenleaf.org/what-is-servant-leadership/.

Without question, a Christ-emulating servant-leader holds a powerful position in his home. Also without question, he selflessly exerts that power for the family's welfare.

Modeling Servant Leadership in the Family

Servant-leadership in any arena, especially in the family, is both sacrificial and costly. Name any metric of personal expense (e.g., money, time, effort): servant-leadership maxes out what is required of the power-holder. Striving to be a servant leader, I must hold loosely those things and activities that pull on me as an individual. Only then am I free to pursue the three servant-leadership outcomes identified in Greenleaf's statement (quoted above):

- sharing power with those I love,
- putting the needs of others first,
- helping those I love to grow and "perform" at their maximum potential.

The apostle Paul illustrated well these servant-leadership characteristics. When addressing one troubling local-church problem, Paul declared his willingness to forego his right to eat as he pleased. Embracing a vegetarian lifestyle, he argued, would be far better than making a *"brother stumble"* (1 Cor 8:13). Servant-leader-type husbands similarly commit to never making their wives (or children) *"stumble"* under their leadership. They prioritize their families' needs, surrendering (as needed) their own life-controlling involvement in the internet, television, sports (participating or observing), or other pastimes. Even an excessive commitment to church activities can compete with effective servant-leadership at home. The more private, personal, and ego-driven an activity, the greater its negative impact will be on the family.

Godly women are amazing! Most are willing to follow their husbands' lead,[12] provided those men are passionately committed

---

12. As in "leadership."

Constantly Applying Biblical Principles

to the Lord Jesus and sacrificially devoted to their families' welfare. Such women willingly play "follow the servant-leader," even if doing so requires a new passport and a tearful farewell to their parents and siblings. In sharp contrast, most Christian women are *not* eager to play "follow the egotistical, self-centered, power-flaunting leader." In the ultimate test of leadership effectiveness, *servant*-leaders win every time.

THE HONORING PRINCIPLE

"Husbands, live with your wives in an understanding way, showing honor to the woman as the weaker vessel, since they are heirs with you of the grace of life, so that your prayers may not be hindered." (1 Pet 3:7)

Peter communicated a mouthful in this high-impact verse. Its powerful directives inform Christian husbanding more succinctly than volumes of non-inspired writing—this book included. Without question, one section in one chapter of one book cannot do justice to this verse. Bear with me, then, as I briefly discuss a few highlights.

Honoring Her *"in an Understanding Way"*

The key phrase in 1 Peter 3:7, *"in an understanding way,"*[13] contains an embedded directive. The adjective *understanding* modifies the noun *way*, implying that a husband must study his wife. He must carefully, thoughtfully consider everything about her. The verse suggests, in effect, that Christian husbands are called to be lifetime researchers: careful observers of moods, cycles, preferences, dreams, fears, and joys. Ignorance is not an option, sir! The expression, "you just can't understand a woman," is a lazy man's excuse for not trying. I am passionately convinced that Peter's style of knowing—true understanding—lies within reach of all diligent

---

13. An alternative, perhaps clearer translation would be *"according to knowledge."*

husbands. *Any* man willing to tune in, watch carefully, and truly "hear" the message between the lines of her communication can understand at least *one* woman!

For various reasons, athletes sometimes start just going through the motions, without tuning into what is happening around them. Whether during practice or competition, observant coaches will often yell harsh directives to such players, such as "get your head in the game."[14] First Peter 3:7 is a call for Christian husbands to get their "heads" in the marriage "game."

After attending carefully to my wife for decades, I *ought* to encounter far fewer emotional trigger points (undetected "land mines") than I did during our first year of marriage. I freely confess I do not always get this research-for-understanding process right. Still, I can testify that living with her *"according to knowledge"* is far superior to living with her in my self-absorbed ignorance.[15] I really dislike painful, unexpected surprises!

Honoring Her in Private, in the Home, and in Public

Peter clearly linked wife-*understanding* with wife-*honoring*; no one can truly honor a stranger! The amount of time I invest in studying my wife (so I can *really* know her) reflects the level of esteem I feel for her. I honor my wife for her devotion to our Lord and Savior, devotion that often exceeds my own. I honor her for the risks she took to become my wife.[16] I honor my wife for her many accomplishments, recognizing that these resulted from hard work and determination, not innate strength or power. I am awed by her amazing ability to transform a house into a home where peace dwells as a welcomed guest.

---

14. Coaches shouted this at me more than once during my high school and college football days!

15. My wife and I have begun using the verbal warning "red alert" to communicate when we are extremely stressed, thirsty, hungry, or exhausted. Red-alert warnings enable us to avoid stumbling unwittingly into active mine fields!

16. Review the section titled "A Bride's Immediate Transformation" in chapter 1.

Constantly Applying Biblical Principles

The knowledge I accumulate about my wife then guides my interactions *with* her; it also informs my expectations *of* her. In other words, I pick my "battles" carefully, based on my diligent study of the lovely "terrain." I learn through attentive observation what threatens her, affirms her, and comforts her. Without this attention to detail, I can easily become angry and frustrated: those ugly near-the-surface emotions that always nullify the *"effective, fervent prayer of a righteous man"* (Jas 5:16, NKJV). Peter's insight into "hindered" prayers is not sophisticated theologizing. Non-angry righteous men get their prayers answered. *Angry* righteous men[17] have pathetic prayer lives: they receive few, if any, answers to their prayers. In fact, they rarely pray!

A Christian husband has opportunity to honor his wife in three distinct domains. In private conversation, he affirms her, meets her needs, and speaks *"tenderly"*[18] to her, as God spoke to Israel through the prophet Hosea.[19] In the home, he honors her through both words and deeds in the presence of their children. And he *never* allows them to disrespect their mother. In public, including the "virtual" public of social media, a Christian husband never speaks disparagingly about women—*especially* his wife! Her dignity is safe in the locker room, the board room, the men's room, and the pulpit. He never embarrasses her, never reveals her flaws, and never, ever exposes their bedroom secrets.[20] Rather, he affirms her and demonstrates the New Testament principle of *"respect to whom respect is owed, honor to whom honor is owed"* (Rom 13:7).

As stated earlier in this chapter, the New Testament sets high performance expectations for husbands. Sir, if you have "blown it" in the past by failing to honor your wife, it's time to man up by kneeling down. Repent to the One who made both of you *"heirs . . . of the grace of life"* (1 Pet 3:7). Then seek the forgiveness and blessing of the one you failed to honor. *Nothing* will work right in your life spiritually until you take both steps . . . on your knees!

---

17. If a man can live in conflict with his wife and still be called "righteous."
18. I like the adverb used in the King James Version: *"comfortably."*
19. See Hos 2:14. See also "Pursuing an Unfaithful Wife" in chapter 8.
20. See the section titled "Exclusiveness Is Seductive" in chapter 7.

THE COLLABORATING PRINCIPLE

"Two are better than one, because they have a good reward for their toil. For if they fall, one will lift up his fellow." (Eccl 4:9–10a)

In this short passage, Solomon illustrated the advantage of collaboration. In almost every arena of life, especially in marriage, two-are-better-than-one collaboration empowers and uplifts. It enables the collaborators to accomplish far more than they could as two individuals working alone.

Benefitting from Collaboration

A wedding-reception toast that includes the phrase "long life" is often prophetic for Christian couples. Recent research,[21] discussed in greater detail in chapter 5, reveals that married couples live longer than cohabiting couples or adults living alone. One possible explanation for this finding is grounded in teamwork. When one spouse feels emotionally low, the other is usually available to support, affirm, listen, and help bear the burden. Rosie and I were new missionaries in 1986. While in Swahili language school, we both experienced brief episodes of the "blues"—striking without an obvious stimulus! This became a fairly common experience for both of us. Fortunately, we were never "down" at the same time: the other was available to offer encouragement, comfort, and sane perspective. The bad days never lingered for either of us, but our gratitude for our spouse's help did.

Marriage is also good for the wallet.[22] The processes involved in setting shared goals and working in harmony toward achieving those goals are financially empowering. Some couples live on one income, others on two. More important than a couple's total income is their willingness to live on the same "page" (of the budget spreadsheet) financially. When two committed people work in

---

21. See, for example, Sander, "Health Benefits of Marriage" (ZLiving).

22. See the section titled "Living with Your Wealth-Conserving Asset" in chapter 5 for additional details.

Constantly Applying Biblical Principles

harmony toward shared goals, they will *"have a good reward for their toil"* (Eccl 4:9).[23]

Finances quickly spiral out of control when spouses no longer share the same goals. The financial impact of divorce, for example, extends far beyond the initial high costs of legal action.[24] If a couple was struggling financially prior to divorce, both former spouses will struggle for years . . . separately . . . after they divorce. Credit ratings *for both* usually drop, ironically at the very time these hurting people may seek additional credit. And the unexpected tax burden created by the sudden access to divorce-settlement income can be devastating for the apparent "winner." The death of collaboration in a marriage demands an extraordinarily expensive "funeral."

Implementing Collaboration

What can husbands do to implement the collaboration principle in their marriages? The business world, specifically the field of project management, offers proven strategies for implementing collaborative partnerships.[25] Implications for Christian marriages are embedded in five secular strategies discussed by Lolly Daskal.

Set Expectations Through Shared Decision Making

From setting deadlines, to dividing tasks, to timing the release of essential communication, ensure that expectations are clear and detailed. Successful collaborators hold each other accountable for commitments.

IMPLICATION 1. Husbands should lead this process of mutual accountability, embracing the goal of performance improvement, not guilt assignment.

---

23. See the TABTO principle in chapter 5.
24. Guillot, "The Financial Impact of Divorce."
25. Adapted from Daskal, "The Extraordinary Power of Collaboration."

Respect Each Partner's Expertise

Complementary skills provide the power for success in any venture. Successful collaborators make major decisions together, dividing the work along the lines of each partner's strengths.
IMPLICATION 2. Husbands should empower their wives to make decisions and to act on those decisions for their families' benefit (see Prov 31:13–22, 24).

Build a Strong Community of Support

Effective collaborators use their connections to recruit a team of helpers. Willingness to seek assistance and expertise, when needed, is a sign of strategic strength, not shameful weakness.
IMPLICATION 3. This recruitment process should include everyone living in the home; in some circumstances, it may include extended family members and friends.
IMPLICATION 4. Husbands must know their limitations and strategically network with others to ensure the success of their families.

Communicate Constantly

Collaborating partners connect daily in order to (1) encourage each other, (2) update each other about actions taken, and (3) plan for the partnership's future. As Daskal noted, "creating a conversation that involves everyone is a great way to build commitment."[26]
IMPLICATION 5. Spouses in a thriving marriage assume responsibility for updating each other often.
IMPLICATION 6. Husbands must ensure that their families' fast-paced living does not interfere with this communication process. They must work with their wives to keep information flowing: spouse to spouse, parent to child, couple to others.

---

26. Daskal.

Constantly Applying Biblical Principles

Share Your Gratitude and Keep It Fun

Collaborators celebrate victories: both the large and the small ones. They celebrate every time something praiseworthy happens through the partners' efforts.

IMPLICATION 7. Husbands should maintain active scrutiny for positive accomplishments within the home and lead the celebration of those "wins."

IMPLICATION 8. Husbands should promote "an environment of gratitude,"[27] knowing that public recognition generates positive energy in the home.

Any partnership will benefit from an enthusiastic commitment to these five principles. Wise husbands understand and value these principles, and the eight implications flowing from them. Those principles and their related implications, when prayerfully applied, will guide and empower their efforts to lead their homes well. Collaboration-oriented homes are marked by far more wins than losses.

LISTEN TO THE LADY: ROLE ADJUSTMENTS AND PRACTICAL SIGNS OF PURSUIT

Whereas the man may have "hunted down" a wife, he now finds himself in a role more akin to a conservationist than a hunter. He must love, protect, and cherish that woman and see to her needs. This includes caring for her emotional "environment." Such caring naturally changes the approach he uses in his ongoing pursuit. Romance is vital, but the day-to-day relationship maintenance in a healthy marriage requires more than just traditional displays of affection. While chocolates and roses may have "worked" during their courtship, marriage requires both partners to determine what kinds of actions are most meaningful in their new stage of life. The definition of what is romantic and what can (again) win her heart must expand past love letters and whispered "sweet nothings!"

---

27. Daskal.

"No woman ever shot a man while he was washing the dishes." I saw this declaration on a T-shirt once and laughed out loud. The message, expressed humorously, conveys a profound truth. Acts of service,[28] such as washing the dishes, caring for the lawn, or occasionally cooking dinner, are practical evidences of a husband's ongoing affectionate pursuit of his wife.

His pursuit should be unending, though its expression may vary over time. Even if a man feels like he married Wonder Woman and thinks she has near-miraculous abilities, she still longs to know that he cares about the little things in her life. A husband must intentionally make time for his wife and seek to discover how he can meet her needs. For a Christian husband, this is the epitome of applying Paul's instruction in Romans 12:10, which urges believers to put the needs of another before their own.[29] Compassion and kindness, when expressed in practical ways, speak volumes to her heart. They let her know she is on her husband's mind, that what is important to her is important to him. His compassion and kindness imperfectly reflect the intimate care of our Heavenly Father for our deepest needs.[30]

I cannot overemphasize the importance of a husband's intentional involvement in his wife's day-to-day, mundane activities. *How can I help you today? Is there anything I can do for you? What can I do to help you with the kids?*—These questions let a woman know that her husband's intentional kindness toward her is still alive and well. He pursues her through his concern about her wellbeing and what is important to her. In so doing, he tends the "garden" of her soul as caretaker of her emotional environment. That husband can expect to watch both his wife and their marriage thrive as God intended.

---

28. See Chapman, *The Five Love Languages*.

29. *"Love one another with brotherly affection. Outdo one another in showing honor."*

30. See Matt 6:25–33.

Constantly Applying Biblical Principles

DEAL WITH IT

Read and View

1. Sander, "Health Benefits of Marriage."[31]
2. "What Is Servant Leadership?"[32]
3. Heitzig, "The Four-Sided Fortress of a Husband's Love—1 Peter 3:7."[33]

Think It Through

1. Which of the four principles discussed in the chapter is most important to your wife? Why?
2. When have you benefitted from the collaboration principle outside of marriage (e.g., in sports, business)? What made the principle work?
3. How does the concept of servant leadership relate to your role as a husband?

Pray It Through

1. Ask the Lord to enable you to find meaningful ways—to *her*—to honor your wife.
2. Ask the Lord for the strength to love your wife as he expects you to love her. Repent for any gross failures to love and treasure her.
3. Pray for (1) divine wisdom to understand your wife more effectively (i.e., in an understanding way), and (2) eager willingness to keep your head in the "1 Peter 3:7 game!"

---

31. https://www.zliving.com/?s=Health+Benefits+of+Marriage.
32. https://www.greenleaf.org/what-is-servant-leadership/.
33. YouTube video: https://youtu.be/FjsHbpVzF3Q.

Act on It

1. View with your wife: "Cultivating Collaboration: Don't Be So Defensive."[34]

    - Discuss how you express defensiveness in your discussions.
    - Discuss specifically how the "red zone" and "green zone" relate to your marriage.

2. Ask her which of your behaviors make her feel honored.
3. Explain to your wife how this chapter has impacted you.

---

34. YouTube video: https://youtu.be/vjSTNv4gyMM.

3

Constantly Pursuing the Moving Target

"The odds of hitting your target go up dramatically when you aim at it."

Mal Pancoast[1]

"Aim not for the target. Aim to hit the target."

Khang Kijarro Nguyen[2]

INTRODUCTION

Greek philosopher Heraclitus was a native of Persian-controlled Ephesus in the 6th century BC. Born a century before Socrates, Heraclitus is best known for his "doctrine of flux": essentially, change is the only constant in life.[3] His insight into the nature of things (and of people) predated by millennia the discoveries of an

---

1. Taken from https://www.quotes.net/quote/58304.
2. Taken from https://www.goodreads.com/quotes/8562285-aim-not-for-the-target-aim-to-hit-the-target.
3. Bryan, "Heraclitus."

ever-expanding universe and the continental shifts occurring on our small planet.

This constant-change maxim depicts well our human experiences . . . and the human dilemma. Relationships are in a constant state of change, as are the relating individuals. Some friendships that once dominated our lives fade into rarely recalled memories. Other friendships thrive for decades despite the major changes impacting those individuals.

Application of the doctrine of flux to marriage is easy. Loving husbands strive to adapt to the "moving targets" wearing their wedding rings, even if those men do not fully comprehend the movement. Aiming to "hit the target" defines the primary test of a thriving long-term marriage. This chapter, seeking to empower husbands to meet this test, addresses four key facts about marriage:

- Change is the only constant in marriage.
- Every husband must come to terms with change.
- Some things that "worked" when courting *will not* work five years later.
- Other things that "worked" when courting *will* work for a lifetime together.

Let's explore this fascinating world of flux!

CHANGE IS THE ONLY CONSTANT

Listen closely and you can sometimes hear their bewildered complaints. After a few years into their for-better-or-for-worse relationships, young married men often struggle to adjust to the transformations taking place in their homes—particularly in their wives. The women they *thought* they knew are rapidly changing, dramatically so sometimes. When speaking transparently with each other, these young (and perhaps not so young) husbands disclose the depth of their confusion:

Constantly Pursuing the Moving Target

- "She's so different now!"
- "She had never told me about that!"
- "I don't know what's gotten into her."
- "We were so happy, focused just on each other. Now she wants ____.[4] I just don't get it!"

These statements exemplify the occasionally honest conversations in locker rooms, coffee shops, and church foyers after the men's breakfasts on Saturday mornings.

The confusion triggering husbands' complaints and bewilderment about their wives often emerge from natural processes of change and growth (i.e., flux). In truth, both husband *and* wife change over time. That loving bride and groom, so blissfully focused on each other during their wedding reception, are *both* in motion. Their trajectories (and the change processes propelling them forward) are not immediately visible. The motion eventually becomes visible, however, sometimes with heart-breaking clarity. Blessed is the couple who discipline their motives, desires, and urges, under Christ's lordship, to move through life *together!*

Change as a universal constant is clearly not constant in its *pace*. In all but the most remote locations, the pace of social and technological change is staggering and accelerating![5] Rapid change creates an environment of social and economic instability that strongly impacts interpersonal relations:

- Jobs once viewed as lifetime careers can become obsolete within months.
- Professionals must constantly adapt and upgrade, or risk losing their credentials *and* credibility.
- Terminated employees sometimes are forced to pursue career changes through further education.

The maxim credited to Heraclitus could now be phrased: "The only thing that is constant is *exponentially accelerating* change."

---

4. Insert here a new interest, vocation, baby, degree, etc.
5. See, for example, Ramirez, "How to Stay Innovative."

COMING TO TERMS WITH CHANGE

Observing change in others, especially in that one person I *thought* was unselfishly committed to meeting my needs, is often easier than recognizing change in myself. Viewing myself as rock-solid stable, the inevitable changes taking place in my wife seem, at times, particularly fast-paced and wide-ranging. Many of those changes are sources of great delight; others, not so much. While I may not have encouraged every change I observe in her, I must cope with *all* of them. To be candid, I suspect that at least *some* of her changes are subtle adjustments to the changes taking place in me. She *will* change, however, no matter what the influence or motivation. How I deal with those changes dramatically impacts my sense of marital satisfaction . . . and her's.

Time Machines Are Dangerous

The *worst* thing I can do is attempt to force my wife back into the pre-changed version of the person she was. She cannot return to that 23-year-old recent college graduate I married last century. My wife is, in small but important ways, no longer that person. Further, I am no longer an unchanged version of the young man she married. (That's why they take photos at weddings.) Trying to shove my wife into a time machine would be a stupid idea, for multiple reasons.

The *smartest* thing I can do is adapt to her ongoing changes and, whenever possible, lovingly encourage them. As spouses, our constant adaptation to the changes emerging in the other will ensure that our individual trajectories remain as interconnected as when we both enthusiastically proclaimed, "I do!" Sir, a wise husband will often confess this to his wife: "I *still* do!"

Growth Is Risky

"Research is risky!" I will never forget that statement permanently affixed to the classroom's bulletin board; I saw that sign three times

Constantly Pursuing the Moving Target

a week while completing my first graduate-level research course. Applicable to many aspects of research, this statement hints at the ignorance[6] that motivates researchers to conduct new studies. They can predict (hypothesize) new findings intelligently but can never know with certainty what they will find . . . until they find it!

Like research, growth is risky. Unlike research, however, growth is not an elective activity. Dynamic growth processes matured two individuals, eventually motivating them to declare publicly their lifetime commitment to each other. Those same maturation processes continue throughout the years (and decades, hopefully) that follow. Human lifespan researchers report that some older couples actually begin to look alike as they grow old together.[7] Sadly many couples do not stay together that long, a fact that underscores the risk inherent in individual growth.[8] If one spouse rapidly grows in a direction not mirrored (at least generally) by the other's growth, their relationship will likely morph in an imbalanced and perhaps unsustainable manner.

Sir, attempting to stifle your wife's growth is as risk-filled as the growth process itself, perhaps more so. As noted earlier, my wife is arguably not *exactly* the woman I married almost five decades ago. She has grown in ways I could never have predicted; most have yielded delightful and intriguing changes that continue to captivate my heart. She no longer desires to direct high school choirs or elementary school music programs. Now she thrives on opportunities to give away portions of God's Word to hurting, discouraged people. She often then prays with them for various needs in their lives. How foolish I would be to resist her growing desire to minister to others in this unique way. My wisest two-part strategy is to (1) commit to grow with her, as I am able, and (2) free her to be the person she is becoming under Christ's lordship.

The woman described in Proverbs 31 was probably an idealized version of a real woman the writer knew; perhaps she was his

---

6. Ignorance is a good thing when it motivates objective, disciplined research efforts.
7. Angelle, "Why Do Couples Start to Look Like Each Other?"
8. See the section titled "Modeling the Process" in chapter 4.

own wife. She likely was *not* an entrepreneurial giant when they first married. Imagine, for a moment, what would have happened if her husband had felt threatened by his highly gifted wife. The book of Proverbs would likely have ended at 31:9!

Unfortunately, the term *threat* describes some husbands' emotional response to their talented, gifted wives. Some threatened husbands, for example, insist on controlling all family income, often to the family's financial detriment. The Proverbs 31 husband was smart enough to let his wife "do her thing." He presumably *encouraged* her growing competence in the interrelated worlds of commerce and home management.

Resisting authentic, Christ-exalting growth simply to reduce its inevitable risk is both selfish and stupid. Let her grow, sir! The self-centered alternative invites only discouragement, relational conflict, and great loss of human potential.

The Seven-Year-Itch Is Avoidable

If it itches, scratch it! Right? Well . . . not always! For example, don't scratch skin traumatized by poison ivy. Don't scratch eczema or chigger bites. And never, ever scratch the itchy "flesh" (Rom 13:14).[9] Should Christian spouses anticipate a "seven-year" itch: a desire for something or someone new? Do previously faithful spouses invariably get "itchy" for more exciting sex after seven years of marriage?[10] Is the life expectancy of passionate marriage *really* limited to seven years (or less)?

A 1955 film starring Marilyn Monroe and James Ewell immortalized the expression synonymous with its title: "The Seven-Year Itch." The movie highlights the impact of non-stop sexual temptation on a husband after seven years of apparently faithful marriage. His marriage (presumably) had become rather dull, perhaps even boring. The point is that our twisted world generally characterizes sex *outside* of marriage as exciting and erotic, while

---

9. "But put on the Lord Jesus Christ, and make no provision for the flesh, to gratify its desires." See also Rom 8:6–8; Gal 5:19–21.

10. "Is There Really a 7-Year Itch?"

sex *within* marriage is depicted as predictable and passionless. Unfortunately, some research evidence supports the latter characterization. In sharp and intriguing contrast, some mental health professionals[11] have reported that sex *within* a Christian marriage can remain passionate, spontaneous, and fulfilling for decades.

The seven-year itch may define some spouses' reality. My conviction? This vow-violating "itch" is an avoidable threat for couples who embrace their individual growth . . . and each other! The lingering impact of those interrelated embraces are delightfully evident in the bedroom . . . and kitchen . . . and living room, etc. The possibility of having sex with someone new is, for many ungodly people, exhilarating. The key, then, to lifelong marital fidelity under Christ's lordship lies in carefully defining "someone new." In important ways, my wife continues to change before my eyes. She is, for me, the best of all possible options. First, she is almost daily someone *new*: exciting and slightly unpredictable because of the changes unfolding in her. She is also someone *safe*: familiar, understandable, and understanding! I find that combination powerfully attractive.

My advice is simple: if it itches, scratch it . . . but *only with your ever-changing companion for life*. Treat all "itches" as catalysts for sexual and interpersonal growth *within* your marriage. Sexual and emotional growth as a couple is possible through transparent dialogue, wholesome books and blogs, marriage enrichment events, and prayer together. These resources allow spouses to honestly confront any "itch" for someone new! The husband and wife who frequently recommit to being that exciting "someone new" for the other really do become that person . . . in ways that matter most to lifetime fidelity and marital satisfaction. Paul phrased it bluntly: *"Because of the temptation to sexual immorality, each man should have his own wife and each woman her own husband"* (1 Cor 7:2). Whatever I might "itch" for, I already have in my wife as we continue to grow together.

---

11. For example, Fisher, "Christian Sex."

WHAT "WORKED" DURING COURTSHIP WILL NOT WORK FIVE YEARS LATER

In most cultures, males carry primary responsibility for the pursuit of a spouse. Without question, females actively pursue attractive potential mates; still, marriage proposals are normally posed by males. Some couples view a marriage proposal as a formality, having openly discussed marriage during the recent weeks of their courtship. In other relationships, a man's marriage proposal truly surprises his beloved. Occasionally, that surprise turns out badly; assumption can be risky! In every case, however, a marriage proposal rapidly moves the couple toward either marriage or the termination of their courtship.

From Courtship to "Ever After": A Fast-Forward Reality Check

A typical courting couple spends extensive (for some, *excessive*) time together. Take two hypothetical believers as examples: let's arbitrarily name them John and Cindy. They love to talk to each other, engaging in wide-ranging conversation about anything and everything. John and Cindy are learning to pray together and to share their personal insights from Scripture. They also are slowly disclosing their most guarded thoughts, desires, and histories. John and Cindy thoroughly enjoy appropriate forms of affection while actively striving to maintain Christ-honoring boundaries. Their behaviors are (1) intentional, not casual; (2) goal-oriented, not conquest-motivated; and (3) increasingly intimate as they envision the future together. John and Cindy just love being with each other . . . so much so that other priorities become demoted a notch or two.

Fast forward five years: married John and Cindy now have a three-year old and another on the way. The countless hours of courtship's *just-us* time have faded into treasured memories. Now, sharing a single fast-food meal with extra fries (a once-favored "dinner date") is neither filling nor all that romantic. Cindy quickly becomes uncomfortable sitting on the restaurant's hard-as-cement benches. Both are focused on their daughter in the play area . . . more so than on each other.

Far beyond her obvious seven-month baby bump, Cindy has changed! While courting, this vivacious, energetic woman wanted to spend every waking moment with John. Back then, she could function on only six hours of sleep during her always active weekdays. Now, she is a weary young mother, trying to decide if she should interrupt her career when little John[12] arrives in a few weeks. Her world now largely orbits around the needs of their children: one romping around the restaurant's play area, the other actively kicking her under the table. Cindy is concerned about how to raise two children simultaneously; she also wonders what impact a maternity leave will have on her career *and* on their family income.

Make no mistake, Cindy loves John deeply and longs for their time together after their daughter is asleep. Still, she knows she is no longer the naturally attractive, high-energy, vivacious young woman she was five birthdays ago. This awareness probably explains the vague feelings of insecurity that sweep over her at times.

From Quarterback to Receiver: A Football Metaphor

Given Cindy's description above, what should John do to pursue his rapidly changing wife? How does he "court" his lover who has little free time, and even less energy? Without question, they cannot return to their previous courtship behaviors. The hours they used to enjoy alone are history. What can John do to win Cindy's heart again . . . and again?

All successful quarterbacks have learned the art of "leading" their pass receivers. This is not leadership in the traditional sense; skilled quarterbacks learn to throw the ball to the point where their receivers *will be* in two to four seconds (depending on the length of the pass). Trying to "lead" his only "receiver," John now does his

---

12. The gender-reveal party was two months ago.

best to *anticipate* Cindy's ever-changing needs, desires, and fears. The phrase "make a pass at her" would take on an entirely new meaning for him!

For at least the next two decades, John and Cindy's "love nest" will be crowded as their little people grow to maturity. Neither John nor Cindy will have the time and energy to recreate their courtship priorities. What previously evoked a romantic evening or a memory-making afternoon together likely will no longer work! Rather than looking back at their history, John should look "down the field" to locate his current moving target. He should then strive to "lead" Cindy, thinking through where she will be (or could be) tomorrow afternoon and acting now to meet her needs then. Perhaps he can rearrange (today) his schedule so he can care for their daughter while Cindy enjoys afternoon tea with her mother (tomorrow). A *non*-Mother's Day card, some unexpected written expression of his continuing love, will likely mean more to her in October than the expected card in May. John can aim to "hit" his loving moving target as often as possible by listening carefully,[13] predicting intelligently, and giving himself sacrificially.

WHAT "WORKED" DURING COURTSHIP WILL WORK A LIFETIME TOGETHER

The major theme of this book is that husbands carry the God-emulating responsibility to pursue their wives throughout their marriages. Our friend John must continue to "court" his wife Cindy even as she grows and changes as a person. Specifically, he must continuously modify (at *least* tweak a bit) those behaviors that allowed him to win Cindy's hand in marriage in the first place. As argued above, the specific behaviors[14] that "worked" during courtship are not sustainable throughout their marriage. However, the *principles* John and Cindy employed during their courtship will work quite well for the decades of marriage ahead. *Behaviors* must

---

13. Review the section titled "The *Honoring* Principle" in chapter 2.
14. And the unsustainable prioritizations that facilitated those behaviors.

change as the couple changes. *Principles*, especially those grounded in Scripture, endure for a lifetime.

Three enduring principles of lifelong courtship are (1) embracing honesty, (2) negotiating conflict, and (3) prioritizing their relationship. Other principles, such as speaking gently and behaving sensitively, are important. These three, however, merit John's special attention.

Embracing Honesty

Many years ago, a recently married woman disclosed to my mother her great disappointment with her husband after only a few months of marriage. The man who had seemed so interested in the things of God, including church attendance, during their courtship had not attended church once since their wedding. This woman felt cheated and betrayed because her husband had not been honest with her. He had, apparently, told her what she wanted to hear, but he definitely had not told her the truth about his less-than-committed walk with Christ.

Honesty always works! It is a foundational principle of long-term marriage. If two individuals give each other ever-deepening self-disclosure during their courtship, the "ground" for post-wedding surprises (even shocks) shrinks. True, John will continue to be surprised by previously undiscovered aspects of Cindy, and she will continue to discover—and rediscover—her husband John. Ask fifty couples who have been married for at least two years to list things about their spouses they did not know at the time of their wedding. Doubtless, all fifty husbands could easily generate an impressive list. And, as argued above, occasional surprises will continue to surface as each of those one hundred spouses grows and changes. Their surprises should, however, rarely shake the foundation of their marriage provided they have been transparently honest with each other.

Sir, honest disclosure is always in your best interest, both before and after the wedding. Undisclosed secrets are detrimental to a growing one-flesh relationship under Christ's lordship. A sinful internet history, a flirtatious relationship at work, or thousands of dollars in credit card debt—once exposed, such previously unshared facts create "shock waves" that can crack the foundation of your marriage.[15] *Keep it honest!* Invite her honest feedback by modeling it. Smuggling secrets into your marriage is a blatant form of wife abuse.

Negotiating Conflict

All relationships experience times of conflict and stress. The more important the relationship, the greater the damage interpersonal conflict can create. Under intense emotional stress, men tend to respond to relational conflict as their fathers did, women as their mothers did. Research in one application of this principle is conclusive: hurt people grow up to hurt other people.[16]

Some men were raised in homes in which one or both parents withdrew emotionally (perhaps even physically) during conflict. Stress-induced withdrawal *always* leaves the stench of unresolved conflict hanging thick in the air. Children easily detect that odor! When grown, now with families of their own, those former boys struggle to stay engaged emotionally and physically in difficult conversations. Their default setting[17] is to run-withdraw, though they may sometimes lash out in trust-shattering anger.

Man-cave withdrawals at moments of intense conflict are, unfortunately, reinforcing[18] because they provide temporary escape from painful situations. Such withdrawals are ultimately self-defeating because the source of conflict is never resolved, certainly not in a relationally healthy way. Wise men do not "cave in" during relational conflict; they manage their frustration, stay tender and open, and keep the conversation rolling. They have discovered

---

15. See the section titled "Pursuing a Wounded Heart" in chapter 8.
16. Askin, "Abusive Partners Can Change!"
17. Set during childhood through the powerful process of modeling.
18. The technical term from the psychology of learning is *negative reinforcement*, as in the humorous statement, "I sometimes hit my head repeatedly with a board because *it feels so good* when I stop!"

that, in the long run, conflict *resolution* hurts less than conflict *avoidance* ... no matter how nicely equipped the man cave.

Many men face the challenge of working through conflict having never seen it done (modeled) well.[19] They may need specific training in couple communication skills. John and Cindy, for example, may need to attend a weekend retreat[20] during which gifted presenters teach and model those skills. Such a retreat could generate both immediate and long-term blessings for their growing family. Watching John and Cindy proactively resolve their conflicts will profoundly impact their children. Those blessed children will learn that parents *can* work through conflict in healthy, relationship-strengthening ways. That life lesson is one of the greatest gifts parents can give their children.

Prioritizing the Relationship

Work is essential. Leisure activities are important. The house and car must stay in good repair. And serving others is a biblical mandate, especially in a local church. But nothing on earth matters as much as marriage. Taking others for granted is a relational sin. Taking your wife for granted is a *stupid* relational sin. I would often caution my children when they were just starting a risky behavior: "Nothing good can come from this!" Eventually, I just abbreviated that warning: "NGCCFT!" This abbreviated caution clearly applies to non-marital relationships and activities that can dominate a husband's life. John should *never* assume that Cindy's heart is still focused on, and tender toward, him. *Don't assume, John: NGCCFT. Prioritize!*

Sir, she was your top priority when you two were courting ... and she knew it! She *still* needs to see that same level of commitment ... daily ... from the man who won her heart. Just as prioritizing your relationship "worked" during your courtship, prioritizing it will "work" for the rest of your lives together. Remind her often

---

19. See the section titled "Pursuing 'Uphill'" in chapter 8.
20. Or pursue marriage counseling.

of this. Show her often that, next to your growing relationship with Jesus, she is still your greatest joy, treasure, and priority.

LISTEN TO THE LADY: INVESTING IN CHANGE

There's a joke that says that the only time a woman can change a man is when he's in diapers. The societal mindset is that men are either stubborn toward change or altogether incapable of it.

But, gentleman, you already *have* changed! It may not be due to any "doings" on your wife's part, but the fact remains that just as she isn't the same girl you married, neither are you the same strapping young man she married. (I'm sorry to break that news to some of you.) You've had life experiences, both good and bad. And the two of you have been affected differently by those experiences. Time has made its own alterations to your body, and both your personality and opinions on important issues have also shifted. Have you considered that your wife may be dealing with a new reality (you!), just as you are?

Are you harder or easier to live with since you first married? Are you committed to improving your marriage by contributing the best version of you that you can be?

Obviously, you're reading this book, so that's a good start, but it will take a lot of work and intense focus to bring a better you to the table, so to speak. Honest self-assessment is in order. What do you do that charms—or alarms—your spouse? What feedback about her changing husband has she shared with you?

We can all quickly justify our own obnoxious behavior, but self-justification is almost never healthy. *"If he/she wouldn't ___ (fill in the blank here), then I wouldn't ___ (fill in the blank here)."*— Such "if-then" thinking prevents you from owning responsibility for your behavior. And the statement, *"Well, that's just the way I am,"* is a poor excuse for inconsiderate behavior. Such statements reflect a lack of commitment to growth, a failure to constantly pursue self-improvement. They also serve as a glaring mark of immaturity, particularly if the behavior is harmful or toxic. Is there

Constantly Pursuing the Moving Target

anything in the way you handle conflict with your spouse that needs an overhaul?

Your wife has changed, for sure, and change is tough! She has changed in ways even she doesn't necessarily like. How can you help her navigate those turbulent waters of "flux"? How can you offer grace and understanding to your changing wife? I have three tips for starters:

- Make an honest self-assessment of your own changes, for better or worse.
- Have courage in the midst of change to intentionally change for the better.
- Initiate a conversation with your wife. How can the two of you work together to honor the changes in each other?

One final thought: Your wife married you because she wants her closest relationship with another being on the planet to be with you. Your relationship is worth every ounce of time and investment you put into it.

DEAL WITH IT

READ AND VIEW

1. Church, "Coping with Change in Your Marriage."[21]
2. Purtill and Kopf, "Happiness Doesn't Change Much in Long Marriages."[22]
3. "Best Throws in NFL History."[23]

THINK IT THROUGH

1. What lessons about marriage can you extract from the football video?
2. In what ways do you handle marital conflict as your father did?
3. In what ways do you respond differently to conflict than your father did?
4. Can a Christian marriage become "itch" proof (as in the seven-year itch)? If so, how?
5. What specific actions or steps would lead to achievement of that itch-proof goal for your marriage?

PRAY IT THROUGH

1. Ask God to help you identify creative ways of prioritizing your marriage.
2. Repent for any abusive or hurtful comments during times of conflict with your wife.
3. Pray for wisdom to know how to handle conflict with your wife as a mature man of God.

---

21. https://smartcouples.ifas.ufl.edu/married/coping-with-problems-and-challenges/coping-with-change-in-your-marriage/.

22. https://qz.com/1315193/how-happiness-in-marriage-changes-over-time/.

23. YouTube video: https://www.youtube.com/watch?v=A_Of0jcpaKc.

Constantly Pursuing the Moving Target

4. Pray for the ability to "tune in" to your wife so *she* knows you truly understand her.

ACT ON IT

1. Read with your wife: Ludden, "How Marriage Changes Your Personality."[24]

    - Do you agree with Ludden's conclusions about changes in men and women after marriage?
    - Discuss both of your answers, recognizing that you and your wife may view change differently.

2. View with your wife: "Broken Together"[25] by Casting Crowns. Share openly how this music video impacts you.

3. Explain to your wife how this chapter has impacted you.

---

24. https://www.psychologytoday.com/us/blog/talking-apes/201803/how-marriage-changes-your-personality.

25. YouTube video: https://youtu.be/RhxELo-uD3c.

4

Constantly Devoted to an Amazing Woman

> "The credit belongs to the man who is actually in the arena, who strives valiantly . . . who knows great enthusiasms, the great devotions; who spends himself in a worthy cause."
>
> THEODORE ROOSEVELT[1]

INTRODUCTION

Devotion: journalists and reporters rarely use this term except during Veteran's Day and Memorial Day ceremonies. The word normally communicates a passionate commitment to an ideal (e.g., devotion to duty) or a cause (e.g., devoted to reaching the lost with the gospel). In a far more casual and largely inappropriate sense, many Christians label their daily Bible reading and prayer time as their *devotions*. They often feel guilty for skipping a morning devotion (a noun), even though their lives are fully devoted (a verb) to Christ.

---

1. Taken from https://www.goodreads.com/quotes/7-it-is-not-the-critic-who-counts-not-the-man.

Constantly Devoted to an Amazing Woman

Some definitions of *devotion* emphasize a strong commitment to another person: for example, "love, loyalty, or enthusiasm for a person or activity."[2] Let's personalize this definition by describing two typical spouses: determined David and amazing Annie. This chapter invites David to *devote* himself to Annie's comprehensive welfare, including her:

- Spiritual growth,
- Intellectual and professional growth,
- Pleasure.

Every husband, even on his best days, reflects poorly God's perfect devotion to his children. Thankfully, a husband's *devotion* does not require *perfection*, only commitment and consistency. A Christian woman like amazing Annie is likely to thrive in marriage if her husband constantly (although imperfectly) devotes himself to the three dimensions of Annie's life listed above. In turn, a thriving-in-marriage woman like Annie is highly motivated to ensure that David, her constantly devoted husband, is happy and content!

DEVOTED TO HER SPIRITUAL GROWTH

Let's continue to explore David and Annie's relationship. His greatest joy and responsibility is to facilitate Annie's growth in Christ Jesus. As her spiritual *"head"* (1 Cor 11:3), David is ultimately responsible to Christ as he strives to fulfill this demanding role. A constantly devoted husband will, in fact, passionately strive to lead in two interrelated processes: their growth as individuals and their growth as a couple. This section briefly explores four "tools" that facilitate David's expressed devotion to Annie's spiritual growth.

---

2. "Devotion" Oxford English Dictionary (https://en.oxforddictionaries.com/definition/devotion).

Modeling Spiritual Growth

Every Christian husband should strive to model the process of spiritual growth. His wife should *easily* observe his daily commitment to growing in Christ. For example, David faithfully reads God's Word and other faith-building literature. And he eagerly shares with Annie his latest insights from that reading and from his prayer time. Over the years, she should easily observe David's commitment to Christ mature and deepen. Blessed is the wife whose husband models the process of spiritual growth.

Facilitating Her Devotional Reading and Prayer Time

A devoted husband knows that his wife needs some "me" time daily: specifically, some "me-and-Jesus" time. A married Christian woman is first a child of God, then a wife, mother, and all the other roles that uniquely define her. David can communicate his commitment to Annie's spiritual growth by ensuring she has uninterrupted time with her Lord daily. For example, he may need to provide child care during this time; freeing her from distracting interruptions must remain a high priority.

Encouraging Her Attendance at Ministry Events

Devoted to his wife's spiritual growth, David will actively encourage Annie to attend ministry events she finds appealing or growth-inducing. His encouragement must be practical: sacrificially investing as a couple in her travel, accommodation, and event registration. David can also facilitate her absence by striving to meet their children's daily needs. His proactive blessing, both before she leaves and after she returns, will help to offset Annie's natural feelings of concern about her family while away. After she returns, his active listening will ensure that the ministry event has maximum impact on her. Determined David will listen carefully as Annie describes what she learned and who she met.

Respecting Her Spiritual Leaders

A devoted husband must exercise great care when discussing their spiritual leaders. No leader is perfect: over time, flaws readily become apparent. Many of those flaws can simply be ignored; others may need to be addressed in some Christ-honoring way. In *every* case, however, David will communicate respect for Annie's spiritual leaders, including her local-church female leaders. In so doing, he will avoid putting her in a relationship-damaging loyalty bind. Few experiences in a woman's spiritual journey are as painful as her husband's disrespect for one of her leaders.

DEVOTED TO HER INTELLECTUAL AND PROFESSIONAL GROWTH

A fully devoted husband welcomes every expression of his wife's competence, even in those areas that expose his own weaknesses. At issue for a constantly devoted husband is *her* growth, not *his* ego. And let's be candid here: a strong, competent woman is amazingly attractive (see Prov 31). Contributing to her intellectual and professional growth is one of the great joys of marriage for a loving husband. David most easily does this by modeling personal growth himself, actively facilitating-encouraging Annie's growth, and affirming her unique gifts and talents.

Modeling the Process

Modeling[3] intellectual and professional growth becomes foundational for one devoted to encouraging. Words of encouragement are far more effective than words of criticism. Still, *verbal* encouragement has its limits; it works best when paired with a credible, manipulation-free, this-is-how-I-do-it example. Paul charged Timothy to emulate his teaching behaviors: "*What you have heard from me in the presence of many witnesses entrust to faithful men who will be able*

---

3. Asatryan, "5 Ways to Get Your Partner to Change."

to teach others also" (2 Tim 2:2). Modeling positive behaviors and attitudes can powerfully bless any wife ... and any marriage.

Growth is *always* risky.[4] Infants know this well: falling hundreds of times while learning to walk is painful and frustrating. Teenagers know it, too: sorting out their place in both the real and virtual worlds can, at times, feel overwhelming. As adults, spouses sometimes struggle with their own intellectual and professional growth. A woman's growth-related struggles seem less daunting, however, if she can watch her devoted husband face and successfully work through his own issues and uncertainties.

By modeling (never demanding) intellectual and professional growth, David will avoid the temptation to "clone" himself in Annie. His related desires are only to inspire and illustrate, not force or dictate. Annie's continuing development and growth are, ultimately, her own responsibility. And the path she pursues in that growth process will be uniquely hers, not a mirror image of his. A devoted non-controlling husband like David simply rejoices in his wife's growth.

Facilitating-Encouraging Her Intellectual and Professional Growth

A fully devoted husband will be vitally motivated to invest in his wife's growth ... as much so as in his own. The marital counseling literature is clear on the importance of *both* spouses growing as individuals.[5] Relationship instability inevitably increases when one spouse embraces rapid personal growth while the other remains relatively static.[6] One couple blogged, "You simply have to be intentional about choosing, learning, and discovering new things about your spouse. So you can grow together, and not apart."[7]

---

4. Review the section titled "Growth Is Risky" in chapter 3.
5. Keith, "Growing Together in Marriage."
6. Slatkin, "How Self-Growth Can Wreck."
7. Marcus and Ashley, "Growing Apart in Marriage."

Constantly Devoted to an Amazing Woman

As argued above, a growing, developing husband like David is ideally positioned to encourage and facilitate (again, *not* demand) his wife's continuing growth. His own growth is vital: this book is intensely focused on his multifaceted growth as a man of God and husband. The related processes of facilitating and encouraging Annie's growth do not require David to sacrifice his own goals.[8]

Affirming Her Unique Gifts and Talents

Affirming Annie's unique gifts and talents, especially those that are not income-generating, may be difficult for David. In some cases, her gifts and talents do not significantly impact the couple's financial "bottom line." Leading the growing children's church ministry at their local church, for example, is normally volunteer work. Even so, David's willingness to focus on their *relational* bottom line will yield huge "dividends" for both of them. Bank account balances are convenient, but ultimately unreliable, metrics of intellectual and professional growth.

How can David affirm-support Annie's personal growth? The four key markers, briefly discussed below, provide ample evidence of his support. Each marker is grounded in, and directly impacts, Annie's *emotional* growth. Few people—male or female—can grow in competence when they are emotionally fragile. Evidence abounds that emotional growth and intellectual-professional growth are inseparably intertwined.[9] A wise, devoted husband like David will ensure that his *emotional* affirmation-support parallels his *logistic* affirmation-support of her growth and willingness to take risks. Both emotional and logistical affirmation-support empower Annie to pursue the full expression of her gifts and talents.

---

8. Note that in many thriving marriages, "Annie" is a highly trained professional and "David" works in a blue-collar trade. This does not exempt "David" from striving for personal growth and welcoming it in his wife.

9. "How Your Emotional Intelligence." See also Sanfilippo, "What Is Emotional Intelligence?"

Investing Family Income in Her Personal Growth

Investments in personal growth may take the form of individual or couple counseling, or possibly life coaching that offers Annie some specialized guidance. Her continued growth may require formal academic training (degree or certificate). If Annie is highly motivated to pursue higher education, for example, David would be foolish to object. A devoted husband will eagerly agree to invest family resources in his wife's growth, knowing this investment will positively impact their relationship.

Attending to, and Respecting, Her Learning Style

Potential mates are often attracted to each other because they do not think alike and, therefore, do not learn in the same manner.[10] For example, Annie may thrive as a field-dependent learner,[11] needing guidance by a teacher or mentor, at least at first. In sharp contrast, David may be a field-independent learner: "Give me the manual and close the door on your way out. I will figure it out myself." These differences in learning style do not reflect a meaningful difference in aptitude or intelligence; preferred learning style and intelligence are *not* significantly corelated.[12] A wise husband like David will never disparage his wife's preferred approach to learning new tasks, aware that she may test higher than him on a standard IQ measure.

Refusing to Pressure Her Toward Goal Achievement

Annie's dreams of achievement will fail miserably if she feels pressured to pursue a goal she does not value, no matter how important that goal may be to David. Those in one-flesh relationships must never assume that *their* personal goals are automatically

---

10. Goldman, "How Men's and Women's Brains." See also Wehrwein, et al., "Gender Differences in Learning Style Preferences."
11. Like "Annie," I am a field-dependent learner.
12. See the two articles by Goldman and Wehrwein, et al. (cited above).

shared by their spouses. A devoted husband like David will validate and affirm *his wife's* goals, even if he could never envision pursuing those goals himself.

Treating Her as an Adult Peer, Not as a Child

This affirmation may require David to privately confront (and repent of) a paternalistic attitude toward Annie. Some husbands, fortunately a minority, speak to their wives (and to others *about* their wives) as though they were children. Such men rarely address their wives as their growing-in-competence peers. Their pathetic attitude reflects not only the disrespect they feel for their wives, but also for the Lord who created those women.[13] In sharp contrast, a devoted husband like David will treat Annie as a treasured companion and peer.

DEVOTED TO HER PLEASURE

I initially labeled this section "Devoted to Making Her Happy She Was Born a Female."[14] I later determined that the word *pleasure* is encompassing and more focused. Women rarely, if ever, thrive in marriages marked by power competition and relational strife. And thriving-in-marriage women are *never* found in abusive relationships! Only a man devoted to his wife's pleasure can encourage her to fully embrace her femininity. His devotion can be expressed in at least five distinct ways: three are positive and should be practiced daily; two are negative and should be totally shunned.

Lavishing Affection on Her

Some men embrace as their role model the legendary "strong silent type"[15] husband. The legend goes like this: under intense pressure

---

13. See also the sub-section below: "Refusing to Disparage Her."
14. I still like that phrase, though admittedly too long for a section title.
15. Also known as "stupid."

from his "nagging" wife, the man blurts out, "I told you thirty years ago when we married that I love you. If I ever change my mind, I'll let you know." In sharp contrast, a "fully devoted"[16] husband may indeed be strong, but is *never* silent! David, our illustrative husband, *often* confesses his ever-increasing, passionate love for Annie. He *lavishes* affection on her: she is the focus of his continuous desire and love. Kisses (both gentle and passionate), tender hugs early each morning, a loving hand on her waist or shoulder as they walk together, soothing words of comfort—*all* are examples of lavished affection.

Every devoted husband must exercise wisdom in his expressions of affection. Sir, what you do to express affection must be perceived-received as just that: *genuine* affection, not sexual foreplay or some twisted form of manipulation. Make it your constant goal to reach her *heart*; her body will follow her heart if you are wise and gentle. I am forever grateful to a female classmate in high school who confronted one of my football teammates with this gem: "holding hands with a girl is never a waste of time." Herein lies great wisdom, oh, devoted husband: what is not a "waste of time" for your amazing wife is *never* a waste of time for you!

Praising Her Verbally

Wives long to hear their husbands' sincere praises. Few ask directly for words of praise; most *deeply desire* to know—and be reminded often—that they please their mates.[17] A wise husband like David will often affirm and praise Annie in public.[18] He will do the same in private: in front of their growing children and (in even more intimate terms) behind closed doors.

Watching their father habitually praise their mother deeply impacts children at all ages. This is, in fact, part of the process

---

16. Also known as "wise."

17. In chapter 3, I recommended occasionally telling your wife "I *still* do" (as in, "take this woman to be my lawfully wedded wife").

18. Unfortunately, some men—pastors among them—publicly criticize their spouses. Such men must repent!

of shaping family values for boys and girls. When father praises mother, his actions demonstrate that women are of great worth. Envision a potentially disrespectful teenager: let's call him Hank. Through unique circumstances, Hank is living in your home for several months. This lad will think twice (or even thrice) before uttering a cutting remark or snide comment about your wife if he hears you . . . often . . . sincerely praising her. A devoted husband's lavished praise and loving admiration become a shield of protection for his wife in both public and private.[19]

Giving Her Physical Pleasure

Whether in a shopping mall, a restaurant, or their bedroom, a wise devoted husband like David will attend carefully[20] to what is pleasurable to his wife. His highest joy erupts as he discovers new ways of giving her pleasure. Caring, creativity, and sensitivity (CCS) to her words and physical responses form a triad of pleasure-giving guidance available to every husband. Sir, I urge you to employ the CCS triad often!

Like most men, David faces a serious challenge in pleasure-giving. He must overcome his default assumption that what brings *him* pleasure will also pleasure *her*. A devoted husband must "tune in" to his wife's mind, body, and emotions. Women often need time to savor the full impact of physical-sexual pleasure. They first need to know they are truly safe: their responses, especially the sexual ones, are both treasured and protected.[21] Time devoted to relaxed foreplay[22] is *never* wasted; this CCS time is an integral part of the sexual experience for most women. Her sexual desire grows

---

19. For example, the husband of the Proverbs 31 woman exclaims, *"Many women have done excellently, but you surpass them all"* (31:29).

20. Review the section titled "The Honoring Principle" in chapter 2.

21. See the section titled "Exclusiveness Is Seductive" in chapter 7. See also the section titled "Refusing to Disclose Intimate Details about Her" later in this chapter.

22. Note the word *play* in this word. Keep your play time *play*ful—for *both* of you!

rapidly in an environment of relaxed—and *totally* private—play and pleasure-giving.

Wife-pleasing sexual intercourse illustrates this pleasure principle: it is, however, only one "thread" in the larger pleasure "cord." Rephrased, pleasure is a much broader category of human experience than just sex. Thus, a husband devoted to his wife's pleasure will strive to please her in the bedroom and elsewhere! For example, David may periodically surprise Annie with some special event that *she* (not he) finds pleasurable. A quiet walk hand in hand on a wooded trail or an hour of personal conversation at a special coffee shop are deeply pleasurable for many women. A couple of hours of pampering in a day spa or beauty shop may also bring her pleasure. And passionate kissing during a tender embrace (kissing that does not always lead to sex) is pleasurably addictive for most women.

When expressing his devotion to Annie's pleasure, David will focus more on her mind than on her body. He is not in a rush to get her in bed. He has learned that her body will generally follow her well-pleasured mind;[23] the reverse *rarely* works so effectively . . . for either of them.

Refusing to Disparage Her

A CCS-type husband devoted to his wife's pleasure will never disparage her or publicly joke about her weaknesses or failures. He will guard his comments about her, whether she is present or not. Relatives in both extended families will hear only words of praise for her. He reserves for their private conversations any frustrations he feels compelled to share.

Unfortunately, some children (like Hank, the teenager described above) speak disparagingly *to* and *about* their mothers in public. A cutting word, a spiteful gesture, or a mocking tone can deeply wound a woman; they leave her feeling verbally assaulted and defenseless. Such offensive behavior by children and teens

---

23. Review the last paragraph in the previous sub-section: "Lavishing Affection on Her."

evidences their fathers' failure; those men have failed both their children *and* their wives! Determined David will *never* allow Annie to be disrespected: not by his own words, and certainly not by the verbal attacks of others!

Sir, the easiest way to avoid embarrassing your wife is to avoid "bad-mouthing" women in general.[24] Silly comments about "air heads" or "dumb blondes," for example, may evoke a moment of laughter from friends. That brief moment of levity comes at a price, however! In fact, the price it imposes is *much* higher than intelligent men would willingly pay. When a boy (like Hank) hears his father ridiculing women in general, he will likely follow his father's example. The resulting conflict and turmoil in the home, especially as that boy grows into a young man, can wreak havoc within the family for years.

In sharp contrast, a wise, devoted husband like David serves as a superb role model for his children. The attitude this CCS-type man displays toward women in general, and his wife in particular, will likely become permanently embedded in his children: both genders. Generally, they will value what their father values, including the dignity of their mother.

Refusing to Disclose Intimate Details about Her

Fear of exposure when vulnerable or defenseless is one the greatest threats a woman can experience. As observed earlier, a woman's ability to enjoy sex is directly linked to the physical and psychological safety she feels in her husband's arms. She may completely shut down sexually if she discovers that her husband has shared with his friends details about her sexual performance. Her heart-wide-open intimacy and the one-flesh commitment she made on her wedding day can both be ripped to shreds by such senseless

---

24. Remember, Ephesians 4:31 states, *"Let all bitterness and wrath and anger and clamor and slander be put away from you, along with all malice."* And Ephesians 5:4 admonishes, *"Let there be no filthiness nor foolish talk nor crude joking, which are out of place, but instead let there be thanksgiving."* These two verses must apply to your conversations with and about your wife!

exposure. Her full recovery, if it happens at all, may take months or even years. Exposure of their bedroom secrets, in fact, violates a wife almost as much as her husband's infidelity or addiction to pornography.[25]

Adultery and fornication are promoted by a what-happens-in-Vegas-stays-in-Vegas attitude. That attitude winks at sexual sins committed away from home. The exact opposite characterizes David's integrity-driven commitment: what happens in their bedroom stays in their bedroom. As a result, Annie feels safe, knowing that:

- Their bedroom door is locked: unexpected interruptions (other than true emergencies) will not be allowed.
- His mouth is closed: he will not disclose intimate details when interacting with others later.
- His cell phone is off: its ring tone will not interrupt them, and its audio-video recording app is not capturing their activity (no matter what the justification or wild impulse).

Annie's passionate response to David is fueled, at least in part, by his proven willingness to safeguard their secret communication. Their children don't know the details, nor do his parents, friends, or coworkers. When pledging publicly that he was "forsaking all others," David meant it! As a result, his devotion to Annie's pleasure is exclusive,[26] and her passionate response to his tender advances constitute his reward for a job well done.

LISTEN TO THE LADY:
CHANGE IS INEVITABLE; GROWTH IS OPTIONAL

Marvin warned in the previous chapter, "Growth is risky." I will add here, "Stagnation is even riskier."

Part of the difficulty inherent in doing marriage well is that the union requires both of you to grow *together* while you continue to grow as *individuals*. But you are responsible for growing

---

25. See the section titled "Pursuing a Wounded Heart" in chapter 8.
26. See the section titled "Exclusiveness Is Seductive" in chapter 7.

with her: spiritually, personally, and otherwise. The amount of time you invest in both personal and relational growth will directly impact both of you.

I totally agree with my friend that modeling growth is essential. Modeling even the *desire* for personal growth will speak volumes to your wife. Change is difficult, so don't underestimate the power of your intentional pursuit of growth to encourage and spur on your wife's growth. As your partner, she wants to see you continue to set goals, pursue those goals, and eventually attain them.

New habits are hard to create, and old ones are even harder to break. Your desire to be the best person you can be will inspire your wife. It will also give her a sense of pride in being married to you. No woman wants a languishing spouse who just passively lets life happen to him! A guy who keeps on getting up, no matter how many times he gets knocked down—that man is downright irresistible! Even underdogs are celebrated when they don't give up.

In 1 Corinthians 9:26, Paul described the intense focus he maintained on his calling. He used two athletic similes to communicate that focus: *"So I do not run like one who runs aimlessly or box like one beating the air"* (CSB). Knowing Jesus and making him known consumed Paul's every waking moment. That's the kind of radical devotion to growth your wife longs to see in you. She wants to know that you support her goals, but also that you've got some compelling ones of your own!

She knows change is hard, so if you try to change something and fail miserably at first, don't get discouraged and throw in the proverbial towel. Persistence and perseverance speak volumes to your wife about your strength of character. Even if you feel like the boxer Rocky Balboa, battered and bruised and *almost* finished, get up! Dust yourself off and try it again.

Finally, let her in on the fight! Talk to her about your wins and losses. Let her be your true partner in life: specifically, in your strategic growth, goal setting, and prayer life. Let her be the confidante God designed her to be in your relationship. Proverbs 31:11 speaks to the safe haven she is meant to be for you. If you value her, and sincerely want to support her growth, let her know both your wins *and* your struggles. Your transparency will enrapture her heart.

We women don't want the strong, silent type as much as we want the honest, transparent type, so show her your heart. In turn she'll know she has a safe haven in you.

DEAL WITH IT

READ AND VIEW

1. Slatkin, "How Self-Growth Can Wreck a Marriage."[27]
2. Wehrwein et al., "Gender Differences in Learning Style Preferences."[28]
3. Crabtree, "Affirming Your Spouse."[29]

THINK IT THROUGH

1. In what ways are you modeling the process of growth for your wife?
2. In your judgment:
   - Does your wife feel affirmed? How do you know?
   - Does your wife feel safe in her own home? How do you know?
3. Why is growth risky in a marriage? What are the benefits of continuing to grow, despite the risks (for both husband and wife)?
4. Is giving non-sexual pleasure to your wife difficult or enjoyable? (Later, explain your answer to her.)

PRAY IT THROUGH

1. Ask God to help you express your gratitude and affirmation for your wife. Pray for specific ideas you can implement this week.
2. Pray God's blessing on your wife, specifically that she will thrive in your marriage.
3. Commit in prayer to model the process of spiritual growth.

---

[27]. https://www.huffpost.com/entry/the-enlightened-spouse-ho_b_4101313.
[28]. doi:10.1152/advan.00060.2006.
[29]. YouTube video: https://www.youtube.com/watch?v=bfJx8N4sy6E.

ACT ON IT

1. View with your wife: Evans, "Non-Sexual Affection."[30]

    - Discuss your thoughts about this presentation.
    - Was his message relevant to your marriage? Explain.

2. Work with your wife to develop growth goals for you as both individuals and as a couple. Focus on identifying goals you two can achieve within three years.

3. Discuss with your wife what you can do to enhance her feelings of safety in your sexual relationship.

4. Explain to your wife how this chapter has impacted you.

---

30. YouTube video: https://youtu.be/XSiw_oTGgZM.

5

Constantly Pursuing the Benefits of Marriage

"Happy is the man who finds a true friend, and far happier is he who finds that true friend in his wife."

FRANZ SCHUBERT[1]

INTRODUCTION

Marriage is an amazing, mutually beneficial institution. Without apology, the first half of this book has emphasized a broadly unemphasized truth: the quality of a marriage generally reflects the quality of a husband's pursuit. A marriage can, I suppose, grow rigid—a wife can grow frigid—despite her husband's best efforts in gentle pursuit. After all, extremely rare phenomena continue to baffle scientists! Exceptions notwithstanding, high quality marriages thrive when happy wives are tenderly, constantly pursued by their fully devoted husbands.

---

1. Taken from https://www.brainyquote.com/topics/marriage.

67

Scattered throughout the first four chapters were indications that happy wives are motivated to keep their husbands happy. This chapter elaborates on those hints, attempting to answer every devoted husband's key question: *Exactly* what do I get out of this pursuit business? This question generally parallels the WIIFM (what's in it for me)[2] question the apostle Peter posed one day: *"See, we have left everything and followed you. What then will we have?"* (Matt 19:27). In reply, Jesus gave Peter several amazing promises of temporal and eternal blessings. Building on chapter 2,[3] I devote this chapter to answering[4] Peter's *"what then will we have?"* query.

The diverse benefits of marriage extend far beyond guilt-free sex with a delightful woman. They directly impact, for example, the accumulation of wealth and years of healthy living (positive longevity). Strong marriages, all other things being equal, are sources of profound, multidimensional blessings for both husbands and wives. A wise man will actively pursue these benefits of marriage, rejecting the delusional thought that any other living arrangement could be equally as satisfying. Four key benefits[5] of marriage are discussed in this chapter:

- Living with your best friend
- Living with your wellbeing guardian
- Living with your wealth-conserving asset
- Living with a charming, sensuous woman

LIVING WITH YOUR BEST FRIEND

In many non-western cultures, marriages are arranged by matchmakers or by extended family elders. Those making the

---

2. Review the section titled "Rejecting the WIIFM Style of Loving" in chapter 2.

3. Chapter 2 is titled "Constantly Applying Biblical Principles."

4. At least partially.

5. See Stanton, "Hidden Benefits of Marriage" for a research-enriched presentation of the benefits.

Constantly Pursuing the Benefits of Marriage

arrangements focus primarily on issues of social status and key compatibility variables. The resulting newlyweds assume, or at least hope, that attraction and friendship will grow over time.

In the West, premarital friendship, not premarital sex, forms the bedrock foundation of a thriving long-term marriage. A couple's adjustment to marriage is far easier if they were first friends, then lovers. Passionate sexual attraction, while certainly important, offers an inferior foundation for a lifetime love affair. Friendship, not sex, holds the key to delightful 50th wedding anniversaries. In fact, research[6] suggests that a "high quality friendship in a marriage is an important predictor in romantic and physical satisfaction." Romance alone cannot sustain a friendship; the reverse, however, is clearly possible.

A Best-Friend Wife

The Merriam-Webster dictionary defines the term *best friend* as one's "closest and dearest friend."[7] Another useful definition of this term elaborates: "a person who you value above other friends in your life, someone you have fun with, someone you trust and someone in whom you confide."[8] In popular culture, the term *best friend* is typically applied to a *same-sex* companion: a person with whom you can be free, transparent, and open. Rarely are husbands and wives described in popular culture as "best friends." But popular culture does not—indeed, *cannot*—define the essence of Christian marriage.

Married to your best friend in a Christ-pleasing heterosexual marriage—this statement may strike some husbands as a novel (perhaps even alien) idea.[9] After all, a guy's "hunting buddy" or game-viewing friend is another man. Let's consider two typical

---

6. Schnell, "The Importance of Friendship in Marriage." See also Gottman and Silver, *The Seven Principles*.

7. https://www.merriam-webster.com/dictionary/best%20friend.

8. https://www.yourdictionary.com/best-friend.

9. Review the statement by Austrian composer Franz Schubert at the start of this chapter.

men: Jack and his friend-since-college Ben. The extensive hours these two have spent together, the long history (and adventures) they have shared, and the transparent openness of their conversations have built a strong, lasting friendship. And they have worked to maintain their friendship during some difficult moments in their shared history.

What, then, of the hours Jack spends with his wife Jill? What of the open conversations *they* share? What of the work they have invested in this most-important-of-all relationship? When Jack is asked by colleagues at work about his "best friend," who immediately comes to mind? Is it Ben, the camouflaged, shotgun-toting guy beside him in the duck blind? What about Jill, the warm, loving woman who adopted his last name and shares his bed? Which friendship is his top priority?

Rebuilding a Strained Marital Friendship

Sir, one of the greatest benefits of Christian marriage is the joy of sharing hours every day with a close friend . . . ideally your best friend. A strained or conflicted marital relationship may make this statement seem ludicrous. Conflict can crush a friendship like ultra-deep water crushes a submarine. Can you rebuild a friendship that has devolved into something toxic or lifeless?[10]

Many friendships ebb and flow throughout their history; they strengthen and weaken over time. Andrea Bonior[11] noted that "it is common (and natural) to have friendships wither away when life transitions shift the relationship." So how can a fully devoted husband *rebuild* a meaningful friendship with his wife? Psychologist Erica Loop[12] offered several particularly useful suggestions for rebuilding (or even building initially) any friendship. All of these suggestions apply to marriage, and all require active pursuit:

---

10. See also all of chapter 8.
11. Bonior, "10 Ways to Make (and Keep) Friendships."
12. Loop, "How to Mend a Broken Friendship."

Constantly Pursuing the Benefits of Marriage

1. *Start small.* You will not rebuild a broken friendship in one marathon conversation.
2. *Apologize.* Give a clear, unqualified apology if you are at fault . . . or even *partially* at fault. Own your offensive behavior; be specific about *your* offense (not her's).
3. *Demonstrate regret.* Express exactly how sorry you are for the loss of your previously close friendship.
4. *Devote special time to the relationship.* Take a trip together or create the time for an intimate friendship outing. This can be any activity you both enjoy and allows plenty of talking time.
5. *Reminisce about shared memories.* Talk about the good times that you two have had or look back through photos of the two of you together.
6. *Give it time. . . give her space.* Mending a strained or lifeless marital friendship cannot happen overnight.
7. *Remember the little things.* "It's not grandiose gestures that make up a friendship over the course of the lifespan; it's the consistency of connecting, no matter how small it sometimes needs to be."[13]

A Final Word (or two) About Your Best Friend

This "word" will be short and sweet: *Never* nurture a best-friend relationship with a female who is not your wife! *Don't do it; just don't go there!* Nothing good can come from that—*nothing!* Solomon did not have a refreshing cup in mind when he wrote *"Drink water from your own cistern, flowing water from your own well"* (Prov 5:15). Three verses later, he interpreted his water metaphor: *"rejoice in the wife of your youth. . . . Let her breasts fill you at all times with delight; be intoxicated always in her love"* (Prov 5:18–19). Sir, this is not rocket science: *no other woman* deserves the

---

13. Bonior contributed this final suggestion.

friendship you have, or can build/rebuild, with your wife. Pursue the *right* woman: she's the one wearing your ring!

LIVING WITH YOUR WELLBEING GUARDIAN

A woman who knows she is deeply loved and safe within her marriage is an amazing gift to her husband. She is a live-in health benefit, *at least* as good as an anti-depressant and capable of extending your life by years.[14] These diverse advantages of marriage, especially for men, are well documented in both the scientific and popular literature. A passionately pursued wife, in turn, blesses her husband with health, wealth, and long life.

This section highlights some of the physical and psychological benefits of marriage. Glenn Stanton[15] summarized recently published research: "married people live markedly longer than the unmarried. . . . married men and women are less likely to suffer from serious illnesses, and when they do, their recoveries are quicker and more successful." Researchers consistently report that marriage powerfully enhances the comprehensive wellbeing of spouses. And, overall, men appear to benefit more than women do from the wellbeing blessing found only in marriage.

Your Longevity Advocate

Married men live longer than never-married men.[16] A ten-year longitudinal study in the UK, now somewhat dated (2005), concluded that the health benefit of marriage may be strong enough to "offset the risk of smoking for men."[17] This is a fascinating finding! Light up her life, not a cigarette, and enjoy a decade or two you might otherwise not have had.

    14. This is true of husbands in general. See the details in the following sub-section.

    15. Stanton, "Hidden Benefits."

    16. See, for example, "Marriage and Men's Health." See also Jacobson, "13 Legal Benefits of Marriage."

    17. Wilson and Oswald, "How Does Marriage."

Constantly Pursuing the Benefits of Marriage

A more recent study in Norway found that the mortality gap between married and never-married men was large and growing.[18] This finding is particularly surprising, given the *overall* increase in life expectancy in Norway over the past several decades. This study affirms current mortality research in the US: men who stay married outlive unmarried men by about ten years.[19] Some might imagine that these findings are a byproduct of mere stubbornness! Having something (i.e., *someone*) to live for is likely a superior explanation.

"*Two are better than one, because they have a good reward for their toil. For if they fall, one will lift up his fellow. But woe to him who is alone when he falls and has not another to lift him up!*" (Eccl 4:9–10).[20] This two-are-better-than-one (TABTO) principle explains, at least in part, the increased longevity for married couples. Loving spouses, for example, encourage each other to seek medical care; most unmarried men do not have such a health advocate in their lives.

Let's illustrate the TABTO advantage using two fictional-but-representative men. Bob, a single 69-year-old man, finally seeks medical care for a life-threatening infection. He does so only after several weeks of gradually increasing pain, hoping he would just "get better." Now alone and gravely ill in a sterile hospital room, he learns that he might die there. His 70-year-old married friend, Bill, contracted the same infection, but has enjoyed a far different outcome. In fact, Bill will only dimly recall that trip to his doctor while attending Bob's funeral the following month. Why? Bill's wife insisted that he keep that appointment . . . the one *she* made for him! In general terms, married people live longer, all other things being equal, because *"two are better than one."* TABTO works, sir! Health demographics and mortality data both confirm what Solomon knew millennia ago.

---

18. Kravdal, et al., "The Increasing Mortality Advantage."

19. "What's in It for Men? The Benefits." This research finding is valid, all other things being equal.

20. Review the section titled "The *Collaborating* Principle" in chapter 2.

Your Psychological Booster

Physically healthy people live longer than their unhealthy friends: that deduction does not demand a medical degree. But what about *emotional* health? Do *emotionally* healthy people live longer than neurotic, stressed, or depressed people? Yes! The evidence is clear and compelling. Researchers consistently report a connection[21] between "anxiety-prone personality" (neuroticism) and "shortened lifespan."[22] Why? For one thing, neurotic people produce high levels of cortisol, a steroid hormone; high levels of cortisol are associated with heart disease and various mood disorders.[23]

Neuroticism causes (or is at least associated with) various threats to physical and mental wellbeing. It often leads to depression, which in turn almost always negatively impacts both life satisfaction and longevity itself. A longitudinal study published in 2008 "followed 1,600 men, ages 43 to 91, for 12 years to examine how those with neurotic personalities fared over time. At the end of the study, only 50 percent of the men with high or increasing neuroticism were alive." This figure contrasted sharply with the 75 percent (or higher) still alive in the otherwise identical non-neurotic group.[24] Neuroticism can be deadly!

Relationship stability and emotional stability correlate positively. TABTO appears to best explain this positive correlation. One journalist concluded that "finding love has been linked to prolonging our lives, improving emotional stability and increasing the opportunity for a more positive psychological state of mind."[25] In fact, a caring, open, growing relationship with a woman you love

---

21. This is technically termed a *positive correlation*.
22. Stibich, "How Anxiety Affects."
23. Portella, et al., "Enhanced Early Morning."
24. Stibich. In his article, Stibich noted that people "who are constantly anxious, stressed, and depressed tend to engage in unhealthy habits. They're more likely to smoke, abuse alcohol and other drugs, and have unprotected sex, any and all of which can lead to life-shortening conditions or accidents, such as an overdose or car wreck."
25. Jacobson, "13 Legal Benefits."

Constantly Pursuing the Benefits of Marriage

increases your serotonin levels: *serotonin is an antidepressant!*[26] Love may not always make you happy, but it probably will make you less depressed.

Sir, your wife can positively impact your emotional outlook. She can encourage you to set and reach healthy goals; she can then celebrate with you when you achieve those goals. Consider the positive impact of the Proverbs 31 woman on her husband: *"The heart of her husband trusts in her, and he will have no lack of gain. . . . Her husband is known in the gates when he sits among the elders of the land"* (31:11, 23). By consistently pursuing your wife, you empower her to guard your comprehensive wellbeing, and to enhance your satisfaction with life.

LIVING WITH YOUR WEALTH-CONSERVING ASSET

This section summarizes the positive impact of marriage on wealth accumulation and conservation. Legal statutes provide multiple financial advantages for married couples. And those in long-term marriages are as well off financially as two people can possibly be. The details discussed in this section consistently argue that a good and faithful wife is a true asset to her husband.

The Legal-Based Financial Advantages of Marriage

One amazing benefit of long-term marriage is evidenced by couples' bank balances. All other things being equal, those in long-term marriages earn more money and keep more of the money they earn. Overall, they enjoy greater financial security than divorced couples or never-married individuals (whether cohabiting or living singly). For starters, the income-tax benefits and related financial advantages are enormous. Here is a partial list of those advantages:[27]

---

26. Jacobson.
27. Stromberg, "What's Love Got to Do with It?"

- Joint ownership of checking accounts, investments, and property offers real savings;
- Married couples filing jointly can often (not always) save on their income taxes;
- Health insurance savings are often greater if a couple can be insured under a single health plan;
- Various financial instruments like trusts can be executed only by married persons;
- Social Security, Medicare, and veterans' benefits can be transferred to surviving spouses;
- Surviving spouses do not pay estate tax after the death of their husbands or wives.

Staying married long-term, in addition to all of its other advantages, is by far the *smartest* smart-money strategy a man can adopt. Is it true that "two can live as cheaply as one"? No! That is a sentimental myth unsupported by home economics data.[28] A married "two" can, however, come *pretty close* to that mythical ideal; unquestionably, they can live cheaper than two unmarried individuals trying to make it on their own, even if those two are cohabiting.

Sir, you are by far better off financially with her than without her. This conclusion remains valid, even if she really enjoys shopping: buying new clothes, investing in her appearance, and purchasing various household goods.[29] By pursuing her heart, you are also pursuing long-term financial stability and wealth, benefiting from an "asset" who offers substantial financial advantages under the law.

The Relational-Based Financial Advantages of Marriage

Marriage demonstrably has a positive, multidimensional impact on a man's finances and net wealth. Why is this so? Wilcox and

28. See, for example, Emily, "The Fact and Fiction Behind."

29. This conclusion also assumes that she does not abuse their available credit!

Wolfinger concluded that "after marrying, men typically work harder, smarter, and more successfully."[30] This marriage-inspired work ethic translates into measurable employment advantages. Married men are less likely to be fired and less likely to quit their jobs in anger. Responsibility tempers emotions. Dedication to their families positively impacts most men's job performance and employment history.

Seeking a better job, potentially with a higher salary, is generally a positive move. The challenge is to do it right![31] Job recruiters and company interviewers are normally attracted to still-employed job candidates. Such job candidates "are more likely to have up-to-date skills";[32] they also demonstrate they are trustworthy and dependable. No potential employer wants to hire someone who may suddenly quit or who repeatedly misses work.

Staying employed while seeking a better job is far wiser than quitting a job in order to "have time to look for something better." As indicated above, a current employment statement strengthens any resume. Stay "the course," sir, even if you decide to pursue a different job. Stated differently, run faithfully the employment "race" you are in, even if you seek a better "track" to run on.

Does marriage create a superior work ethic on the job, or do men with a superior work ethic actively seek to marry? Without debate, a high, positive correlation exists between a superior work ethic and a long-term marriage. But which *causes* the other? One university researcher argued that marriage changes men (and their attitude toward work); he rejected the possibility that "happier, healthier, and wealthier men" were simply "more likely to get married in the first place."[33] Sir, marriage will change you . . . almost always for the better! Cooperate with its persistent positive influence. Pursue marriage . . . or stay married. Embrace the change marriage can create *in* you and *for* you.

30. Wilcox and Wolfinger, "Hey Guys, Put a Ring on It."
31. J. Smith, "The Dos and Don'ts of Job Searching."
32. Autenrieth, "10 Tips on Effectively Looking."
33. "Why Are Men Overlooking the Benefits of Marriage?" This report cites key research by Wolfinger.

Do the Math!

Some demographic studies, summarized by Wilcox and Wolfinger,[34] have found that married men make about $16,000 a year more than their single peers with similar backgrounds and qualifications. Focused on older men during their peak earning years, Quentin Fottrell found an even greater income disparity. He reported that, on average, married men[35] earn more than "$80,000 per year." That level of income dramatically outpaced all other categories of older wage earners: they "barely graze $50,000 per year").[36] You can easily do the math!

My mother graduated from a two-year business school but didn't work outside the home after marrying my father. She focused, instead, on raising us four children and supporting our father, a longshoreman who worked long hours in a dirty, dangerous environment.[37] One of her hobbies was couponing: cutting out, organizing, and using coupons for almost everything she bought. She was really good at it, too! At dinner, my mother would often report how much she had saved that day with coupons. My father would often exclaim, with laughter: "Darling, you save me so much money I can't afford it!" I loved that family joke, and I now treasure the math principles it taught me. Two *really are* better than one! My parents' *always*-positive single-income bank balance consistently illustrated Solomon's TABTO truth.

Money is a terrible motive for marrying the woman you love! Money is, on the other hand, a terrific fringe benefit of marriage. Sir, she may not make you rich, but she likely will increase, not decrease, your net worth during your long-term marriage. And if that marriage involves living for decades with a sensuous woman, so much the better!

---

34. Wilcox and Wolfinger, "Hey Guys."

35. Other demographic groups often studied include married women, never married men, and divorced men.

36. Fottrell, "Married Men Earn More."

37. Review the Preface in the front matter.

Constantly Pursuing the Benefits of Marriage

LIVING WITH A CHARMING, SENSUOUS WOMAN[38]

And now for the *really* fun advantage: sex! But not just sex—*charming, sensuous, joyful* sex! A recent article written from a Christian perspective stated well the case for marital sexuality, reflecting previously published research: "Men are more sexually satisfied when they are in a lasting relationship because both spouses are making long-term investments in intimacy."[39] This conclusion, jarringly contrary to popular opinion, may seem incredible at first glance. After all, the message relentlessly "preached" in this commitment-fearing culture is that great sex ends at the marriage altar. In reality, it only starts there.[40] And, as detailed in this section, even secular research data proves it!

A loving wife will, sooner or later, tend to see herself as her husband sees her.[41] If he treasures her presence in his life, she will tend to treasure herself. If he gently pursues her, seeking again and again to win her heart, she will thrive in his love. And if he reinforces her efforts to be charming and seductive, she will eagerly strive to be attractive in his eyes and responsive to his advances. His gentle, consistent pursuit is neither cold behavior modification nor selfish manipulation. This is marriage as God intended it to be: two becoming one flesh, the marriage bed undefiled, hearts united, and love thriving with God's blessing on it.

Reflecting older research findings,[42] one article reported that "51 percent of married men reported they were extremely emotionally satisfied with sex, compared to 39 percent of cohabiting men and 36 percent of single men."[43] In short, the best research findings available clearly suggest that married men have more enjoyable sex lives than either single or cohabiting men. This

---

38. See all of chapter 7: "Constantly Seducing."
39. "What's in It for Men? The Benefits."
40. See Walsh, "Why Religious Married Couples Are Happier."
41. "Johnny Lingo" (a YouTube video).
42. But unchallenged by more current findings.
43. "Why Are Men Overlooking the Benefits?" (ScienceDaily)

marriage advantage is even sharper for younger married men. The Pew Research Center[44] reported in 2006 that 43 percent of those husbands indicated they were "very happy" with life, compared to 24 percent of unmarried men.

The joy of living with a charming, sensuous woman: that is a marriage advantage a man should never take for granted! More than extended life, good health, or accumulated wealth, high (i.e., highly positive) marital satisfaction depends upon and reflects a husband's constant pursuit of his wife. Blessed is the deeply satisfied man who pursues diligently the woman he loves. And blessed is the woman he pursues!

LISTEN TO THE LADY: INVESTING TIME, NOT JUST SPENDING IT

It comes as no surprise that we live in a busy world. Constant pressures and demands can wreak havoc on our most valuable relationship: the one with our life partner. Your marital relationship is only as healthy as the time and effort you pour into it.

God gave you your wife, just as he gave you to her. Your relationship then becomes a gift to you both. Any treasured gift requires upkeep and maintenance; it requires not only your best intentions, but also your active follow through.

The list of suggestions by psychologist Erica Loop[45] on how to rebuild a friendship is worth reviewing and mulling over. In particular, I want to comment on her fourth suggestion: *Devote special time to the relationship.* Success here is as much about how you go about this as it is choosing to do this. As with many things in life, the *why* and the *how* matter just as much as the *do*.

My husband, as wonderful as he is (and he is wonderful), started our dating relationship like any other doting boyfriend. We were both broke college students at the time. At one point, I shared with him my deep frustration about my dirty car. Feeling

44. "Are We Happy Yet?"
45. Loop, "How to Mend."

overwhelmed with my schedule, the car was just one more irritating thing on my long "to do" list. He sympathized in the moment and let me just talk.

A few nights later, he asked to "borrow" my car. Instead of running an errand, he had my car washed and detailed. He then explained, "I know I don't have the money for us to go on a nice date right now, but I wanted to do this for you. I hope it helps." *Um, you bet it did!* I still hold this memory as one of the sweetest gestures anyone has ever done for me.

Fast forward almost a decade into our marriage. We realized we needed to do some reprioritizing to intentionally spend more time together. We agreed to set aside one night a week as *our* night; neither of us was allowed to make conflicting plans. Sounds great, right? It was, until I noticed a predictable pattern emerging. The conversations about date night went like this:

- Me: "What are we doing for date night this week?"
- Him: "I don't know. What do you want to do?"

This brief exchange may seem innocuous, but week after week, month after month, this passivity became aversive. To me, it implied that he didn't want to put any thought into our date nights; I wondered if they had simply become obligations to him. I didn't want to always do exclusively what I wanted. More importantly, I didn't want to be the only one making plans. I wanted his thoughtful attention as much as his good intention. I wanted his leadership and partnership. We eventually made a plan to make a plan *together!*

So yes, Mr. Husband, devote time to your wife, but be an active participant in whatever you do as a couple. It will remind her that you still treasure God's beautiful gift to you.

DEAL WITH IT

READ AND VIEW

1. Stanley, "Why Men Resist Marriage Even Though They Benefit the Most from It."[46]
2. Wilcox and Wolfinger, "Hey Guys, Put a Ring on It."[47]
3. Wilcox and Wolfinger, "Men and Marriage: Debunking the Ball and Chain Myth."[48]
4. "Johnny Lingo."[49]

THINK IT THROUGH

1. What changed inside Johnny Lingo's wife? In what way is this video relevant to your marriage? Be specific. Is your wife an "8-cow" woman to you? Does she know this?
2. Which of the advantages of marriage for husbands discussed in this chapter was most surprising or stood in sharpest conflict with your pre-reading beliefs?
3. In what specific ways might your marriage add years to your life? What changes in lifestyle (e.g., risky behaviors, distain for doctors) would likely enhance your longevity?
4. Popular culture often depicts marital sex as boring and passionless. Why, then, do so many Christian husbands report high levels of sexual satisfaction in their marriages?

---

46. https://ifstudies.org/blog/why-men-resist-marriage-even-though-they-benefit-the-most-from-it/.

47. https://www.nationalreview.com/2017/02/marriage-benefits-men-financial-health-sex-divorce-caveat/.

48. https://ifstudies.org/wp-content/uploads/2017/02/IFSMenandMarriageResearchBrief2.pdf.

49. YouTube video: https://www.youtube.com/watch?v=pfahoLfrddU.

Constantly Pursuing the Benefits of Marriage

Pray It Through

1. Pray for guidance and wisdom to know how to strengthen (or rebuild) a deep, transparent friendship with your wife. As needed, ask God to forgive you for those times you have failed to show her respect.
2. Seek God for creative ways to show your wife how truly valuable she is to you.
3. Pray for wisdom and courage as you determine to avoid nurturing or encouraging all inappropriate friendships. If need be, repent for any too-close friendship you have developed with a woman other than your wife.
4. Thank God for your wife; commit in prayer to continue your gentle-constant pursuit of this great treasure in your life.

Act on It

1. View with your wife: Gottman, "Making Marriage Work."[50] Then discuss the concepts of "masters" and "disasters," with reference to friendship in your marriage.
2. Read aloud with your wife: Schnell, "The Importance of Friendship in Marriage."[51]
   - Schedule time with your wife to focus just on reading this article.
   - Explore each of your perspectives about friendship in marriage.
3. Purchase (or borrow) and begin reading together (aloud, to each other) one of the following books:
   - Gottman, John M., and Nan Silver. *The Seven Principles for Making Marriage Work*. New York, NY: Harmony. 2015. ISBN: 978-0553447712 (320 pages)

---

50. YouTube video: https://www.youtube.com/watch?v=AKTyPgwfPgg.

51. https://psychcentral.com/blog/the-importance-of-friendship-in-marriage/.

- Stanton, Glenn. *The Ring Makes All the Difference: The Hidden Consequences of Cohabitation and the Strong Benefits of Marriage.* Chicago, IL: Moody. 2011. ISBN 978-0802402165 (152 pages)

- Thomas, Gary. *Sacred Marriage: What If God Designed Marriage to Make Us Holy More than to Make Us Happy?* (Rev. ed.) Grand Rapids, MI: Zondervan, 2015. ISBN 978-0310337379 (272 pages)

- Waite, Linda J., and Maggie Gallagher. *The Case for Marriage: Why Married People Are Happier, Healthier, and Better off Financially.* New York, NY: Broadway. 2001. *ISBN 978-0767906326 (272 pages)*

4. Explain to your wife how this chapter has impacted you.

6

Constantly Pursuing Effective Parenting

"Every father should remember one day his son will follow his example, not his advice."

CHARLES KETTERING[1]

INTRODUCTION

Every month, almost always on the 1st, I take pen in hand and write a loving note to my adult daughter. I never plan in advance what I will write; I just want her to know my heart, to let her take the "pulse" of my soul each month. Her feedback is almost never about the details in those monthly epistles. Yet I know she treasures them: she saves each ten-minutes-a-month record of father-to-daughter honesty, disclosure, encouragement, and blessing.

What consistently surprises me is my wife's response to those notes. (I encourage her to read each one before I mail it.) She always expresses how grateful *she* is that I write our daughter. At

---

1. Taken from https://www.success.com/13-loving-quotes-about-fatherhood/.

face value, I am pursuing my daughter by writing her monthly. I want her to know that I love her and remain committed to her welfare. Yes, she is a highly skilled professional woman who owns her home. Yes, she earns *far* more than her father does. And, yes, she still needs to "hear" her daddy's written "voice" monthly! At a deeper level, I am also pursuing my wife through those notes. Few things in life touch her heart as profoundly as our daughter.

This chapter may, at first glance, appear to be off target. After all, the book's title references a *husband*, not a *father*! But the two roles are designed by God to be complimentary. No responsible wife with offspring (aka, *mother*) wants 100% of her husband's time, love, effort, and devotion. She wants him to love her *and* their children.[2] My wife's gratitude for a love note not addressed to her amply illustrates this principle for me.

The interrelated topics addressed in this chapter focus on raising children who are fully empowered to find their place in the world. The long-range goal of parenting is the successful launch of young adults who are willing and able to:

- Get along well with others,
- Value marriage,
- Respect themselves and their parents.

Constantly pursuing effective parenting yields a priceless heritage.[3]

RAISING RELATIONALLY COMPETENT CHILDREN

This section highlights one of the greatest goals of parenting. Launching well the next generation of adults requires parents who

---

2. This is particularly important in a blended marriage-family: a woman needs to know that her biological children are welcomed, valued, and safe in her new husband's presence.

3. This chapter is written to fathers in general, principally to those men still living in harmony with their wives: their children's biological mothers. Creative adaptation of the principles discussed in the chapter will be essential if divorce or separation has ruptured the original nuclear family. See "Pursuing Peace with Your Former Wife" in chapter 8 for additional perspective.

are able and willing to teach and model relational competence through effective communication.

When Relational Competence Is Lacking

Occasionally, news headlines report a sensationally gruesome[4] case of abuse or murder. Media sources label the perpetrators "sociopaths" or "psychopaths,"[5] and their crimes are normally described as "cold-blooded." Capable of shocking violence, sociopaths typically display a complete lack of remorse when eventually apprehended. When violent madness is focused on one's own family members, the term *familiopath*[6] might better connote the perpetrator of the resulting destruction.

No loving parent sets out to raise a sociopath. For example, if Sue Klebold had been asked in 1998 what dreams she had for her son Dylan, she *never* would have replied "mass murderer at Columbine High School."[7] Like this still-grieving mother, most parents—constantly pursuing fathers in particular—long to see their adult children thriving in life, especially in their intimate relationships.

The Family and Social-Relational Competence

The term *social competence* has a long history in the behavioral and social sciences. This term depicts a constructive, even admirable, skill set. Those skills, however, stand in stark contrast to the

---

4. See, for example, Novini, "'With My Bare Hands.'"

5. Reporters may use those terms to distinguish the "senseless" motivation for horrific acts from "hot-blooded" spontaneous motivations, such as road rage or alcohol-fueled bar fights.

6. OK, I just invented this term!

7. O'Connor, "What a Columbine Shooter's Mom Wants You to Know." Sue Klebold reported in her book, *A Mother's Reckoning: Living in the Aftermath of Tragedy*, that the parents of school shooters are almost always overwhelmed by life-destroying emotional pain and regret. They typically attempt to retreat from the public eye when not embroiled in the seemingly unending court cases, both criminal and civil, that plague their lives.

destructive, manipulative skills employed by sociopaths. Public school educators have for decades fostered and reinforced social competence as a desired outcome.[8] A more recently coined term, *relational competence*, usefully explains key dynamics in long-term relationships, including friendships, marriages, and families.[9]

Relational competence, like its first cousin social competence, is a family issue long before it becomes a learning outcome in formal education. Relationally competent families create safe, healthy environments for all of their members. They are generally happy places: homes in which laughter is far more common than crying, hugs are more frequent than fights, and honest conversations—not icy silence or screaming tantrums—characterize family interactions. Relationally competent parents, while not perfect, are *never* intentionally manipulative, harsh, threatening, or demanding. Children growing in such homes learn how to negotiate, wait, take turns, apologize, and trust their parents.

Fostering Relational Competence in Children

How can a loving father effectively pursue the development of relational competence in his children? Striving to be relationally competent himself is essential; no one can effectively teach a skill he does not (or cannot) model. Beyond this foundational competence, the five specific "grade A" suggestions[10] offered by Gary Chapman[11] provide guidance for nurturing relational competence in children. Men committed to raising relationally competent sons and daughters will strive to master these five skills:

1. *Affection.* "It's our job to fill our children's emotional 'tanks' with the affection they need to fuel them through the challenging days of childhood and adolescence."

---

8. "Social Competence."
9. Ngu and Florsheim, "The Development of Relational Competence." See also L'Abate, et al., *Relational Competence Theory.*
10. Yes, all five suggestions start with the letter "A."
11. Chapman, "Raising Socially Competent Kids."

2. *Appreciation.* "Look for ways to thank your spouse and children every day. . . . Training your child to think, speak and even text gratefully begins at home."
3. *Anger management.* "Start by listening. . . . let your child express anger. Concentrate on the reason your child is angry, not on the way he is expressing it."
4. *Apologies.* "If a child hears Dad apologizing to Mom because he raised his voice at her and then hears Mom forgive him, that's a powerful lesson. And parents who sincerely apologize to children not only demonstrate what an apology looks like but also increase the child's respect for the parent."
5. *Attention.* "Boost your child's ability to pay attention. . . . Practice long conversations with questions and thoughtful replies. Eye contact is essential. . . . When you insist upon eye contact and give it generously, you help your child focus relationally on others, even increasing his ability for empathy."

Sir, promoting relational competence is not a complicated task. No complex formulas are needed, just commitment to two relational basics: (1) modeling appropriate behaviors, and (2) teaching how to respond to others in the family in a patient, Christlike way. This two-part commitment will normally result in your children valuing marriage as much as you and your wife do.

RAISING CHILDREN WHO VALUE MARRIAGE

Marriage is really good for children! Research strongly supports this seems-so-obvious conclusion. David Ribar summarized massive research findings in this way: "Children who are raised by their married, biological parents tend to be healthier (both mentally and physically) and do better in school than children who are not raised within marriage."[12] This section explores Ribar's fascinating conclusion.

---

12. Ribar, "Children Raised Within Marriage." See also "Marriage Benefits Children."

The Power of Modeling

The persistent and (hopefully) positive influence of mother and father shapes the worldview of their children in profound ways. Through observation and modeling, children learn that marriage works. They watch closely as Mom and Dad work through their unique difficulties while still generally enjoying life together. Much more is "caught" during eighteen or so years than could ever be directly taught. Children raised in stable, mostly conflict-free homes tend to value marriage and view it as normative.

Ken Canfield[13] urged men to include loving their wives in their parenting strategies. A well-loved and deeply valued wife (also known as "Mommy") becomes a powerful "show and tell" lesson for her children. Canfield advised, "Daily expressions of affection for your wife will do wonders for your marriage, but your children also pick up on it. . . . if the atmosphere of the marriage is love, the whole family will absorb that love."

If Husband Henry dearly loves Wife Wilma and consistently treats her with respect and tenderness, Daughter Debbie will learn this is how it normally works between men and women. What kind of man will Daughter Debbie (almost instinctively) search for . . . and long for . . . as she grows older? The answer to this vitally important question is easy to predict.[14]

And what of Son Sammy? He also will grow to know (almost instinctively) that a man treats the *one* woman in his life with respect and tenderness. The (non-toxic!) masculinity Son Sammy observes during his first two decades will powerfully shape his adult behavior . . . for the rest of his life. Expressions such as "like father, like son" and "the apple doesn't fall far from the tree" visually depict the power of parental influence. Husband Henry should strive to be the father his son will gratefully strive to emulate!

---

13. Canfield, "What Children Gain."

14. The answer is also easy to predict if her father, Husband Henry, regularly cheats on her mother, Wife Wilma. Daughter Debbie will learn that men cannot be trusted, and that marriage is inherently deceptive, uncertain, and unstable.

Constantly Pursuing Effective Parenting

Sir, your children (both genders) need a positive masculine role model: a *real* man who patiently, tenderly, consistently loves their mother! The statement attributed to author H. Jackson Brown powerfully summarizes the dominant message of this chapter: "Life doesn't come with an instruction book; that's why we have fathers!"[15]

The Pain of Divorce and Separation

When I was a child, divorce was a fairly rare phenomenon. Most of my classmates did not struggle with the tsunami of grief and relational devastation created by divorce. Sir, your children live in a different world. A painfully large percentage of your child's classmates, approximately 50%,[16] have experienced, will experience, or are still suffering through, divorce's destructive rupture. Your child may be among them. If so, your challenge to parent well that future adult (hopefully a loving future husband or wife) is even greater.

Canfield, cited above, offered solid advice for parents in general, but especially for those who are parenting in the contexts of divorce and blended families. His short article[17] is a worthwhile read. Sir, if you find yourself in this less-than-desirable situation, *do not* allow your pain to drive you away from your children . . . or your children away from you.[18]

RAISING CHILDREN WHO RESPECT THEMSELVES . . . AND THEIR PARENTS

Some parents believe that if their children simply obey what they command, their parenting task is successful. This section

---

15. Taken from https://www.azquotes.com/quote/678077.
16. Parker, "Key Statistics About Divorce."
17. Canfield, "What Children Gain."
18. See the section titled "Pursuing Peace with Your Former Wife" in chapter 8 for parenting suggestions when fathers are divorced or separated from their wives.

challenges that belief, inviting fathers instead to discipline their children without anger, striving to raise them to respect themselves as emerging adults. Such young adults will almost always respect their parents; obedience for them comes from the heart, not from fear of punishment.

Sowing Respect, Harvesting Obedience

"Children, obey your parents in the Lord, for this is right. 'Honor your father and mother' (this is the first commandment with a promise), 'that it may go well with you and that you may live long in the land'" (Eph 6:1-3). The apostle Paul cited the fifth of the Ten Commandments (Exod 20:12) in his admonition to children in Ephesus; he did this to underscore how important it was for them to treat their parents well. Why? Apart from the threat of force, none of us, children or adults, willingly obey those we do not respect. Some believers may obey their parents simply out of fear of God, but their obedience is joyless.

Paul immediately followed this child-focused command with a strong directive to fathers. His command to children would, apparently, be tough to obey without this follow-up command: *"do not provoke your children to anger, but bring them up in the discipline and instruction of the Lord"* (Eph 6:4). God-honoring *"discipline and instruction"* do not provoke anger—probably because they are not *delivered* in anger. Whatever Paul envisioned by the word *discipline,* it was not linked to anger. Stated bluntly, God-honoring discipline does not provoke anger because the disciplinarian is not angry when delivering it.

Distinguishing Anger and Firmness

Children who respect themselves almost never *disrespect* their caregivers: those who discipline them. One author observed that "discipline means to teach or to train, not to punish. . . . Studies have shown that positive discipline is a lot more effective and longer lasting than punitive strategies."[19] The heart of a loving father is turned in compassion and tenderness toward his child.[20] A heart-turned father can discipline his child without threatening that child's emerging sense of self-respect. *Firm* is a welcomed four-letter word; *anger* is neither!

As a disciplinarian, I was at my best when I was firm, not angry . . . clear, not demeaning. My children needed me to teach them right from wrong, honesty from dishonesty, consideration from selfishness. I didn't always get the *anger*-less part right, to my continuing regret. In saner moments, I knew that my anger interfered with, never reinforced, my overall objectives for my two children.[21] As a truly loving parent, I should have often accepted and acted on my own parental instructions: "Now say you're sorry!"

Fostering Self-Respect

Angela Pruess offered three easily grasped strategies for fostering self-respect in children:[22]

Show Unconditional Love

A loving father teaches and then enforces "boundaries or limits," but does so with love and acceptance. That father makes it easy for his children to obey him. He also makes it easy for them to believe in a loving heavenly Father.

---

19. "Teaching Kids Respect."

20. The angel Gabriel promised elderly Zechariah that his not-yet-conceived son John would *"turn many of the children of Israel to the Lord their God, and he will go before him in the spirit and power of Elijah, to turn the hearts of the fathers to the children, and the disobedient to the wisdom of the just, to make ready for the Lord a people prepared"* (Luke 1:16–17).

21. My dominant goal when raising my two children was to never do anything to interfere with their understanding of a loving heavenly Father. With all my heart, I did not want to pollute their relationship with him.

22. Pruess, "Raise a Responsible Kid."

Teach Your Children They Have Value Without Performance

A loving father consistently affirms his children's "intrinsic worth as people—outside of achievements." He knows that self-respect emerges naturally out of such parental affirmation. Grades in school should never become a battle ground in the home: no one wins a grade "war."

Teach Accountability

A loving father guides his children and holds them accountable when they make mistakes. Rather than "fixing" a difficult situation himself (which often would be much faster), a loving father will hold his child accountable . . . at an age-appropriate level. He will insist that the child develop and implement a plan to set things right. A growing problem-solving ability builds both self-respect and self-discipline.

Let's be clear: parents carry the responsibility to discipline their children. Some do so in anger, and often reap anger or defeatism[23] in return. Other parents have found creative ways to discipline their children, ways that do not involve anger . . . at least normally. Social worker Janet Lehman[24] shared a fascinating observation about one creative approach to child discipline:

> One of our friends was excellent at this particular parenting skill. He would pull his kids aside, say something quietly (I usually had no idea what it was), and it usually changed their behavior immediately.

Lehman then advised, "you don't need to shout at them or embarrass them." Instead, you can take your misbehaving children to a quiet place[25] and "give them a clear message of what is acceptable." If your child doesn't respond to that instruction, you

---

23. *"Fathers, do not provoke your children, lest they become discouraged"* (Col 3:21).

24. Lehman, "Do Your Kids Respect You?"

25. A place away from distractions—especially other children—where they can focus on you.

Constantly Pursuing Effective Parenting

can follow through with an undesirable consequence, but only "if necessary." Threats are *never* effective; appropriate consequences, administered with anger-free respect, almost always are.

Children who respect themselves normally have no difficulty respecting others, including their parents. Stated in reverse, the surest way to receive respect as a father is to model respect-giving by lavishing it on your child. Psychologist Jim Taylor[26] noted, however, that you must remain firmly in "father" (not "friend") mode: "Your children don't want to be friends with you. When I ask children how they feel about being friends with their parents, they look at me as if I'm from another planet. It's just not in their mindset to be friends with their parents." And that "friend" mindset is never encouraged in Scripture.

Sir, your children need a man of gentle strength and transparent integrity to guide them as they grow. They need a man to help them discover how to find their way in the world. They need a man who models self-discipline and self-respect. In short, they need you, sir. Be the man!

LISTEN TO THE LADY: THE IMPORTANCE OF FATHERS

If you turn on your TV during prime time in the US and watch almost any sitcom, you'll note that the dads get the short end of the stick. They are often portrayed as incompetent, emotionally ignorant, or unneeded. Many times, they are absent altogether—"deadbeat dads"—leaving the competent, independent single mom to raise her children as best she can.

If entertainment reflects our society, it's possible the absence of fathers in many households has contributed to this damaging representation. It may also be the result of the feminist movement that holds all men responsible for the actions of a few. The root cause of this disrespect may be debated, but the fact remains that fathers are rarely portrayed in a positive light.

26. Taylor, "Parenting: Respect Starts at Home."

The Christian Husband's Handbook

Ditta Oliker,[27] in "The Importance of Fathers," argued that key social and historical factors explain why the importance of fathers has been downplayed in society. She noted, "It's only recently that domestic courts, recognizing the research on parenting and fathers, have moved to greater equal child custody decrees." Regardless of how society views fathers, Oliker concluded that:

> Fathers do play an important part in their children's lives: the majority of studies affirm that an involved father can play a crucial role, particularly in the cognitive, behavioral, and general health and wellbeing areas of a child's life; having a positive male role model helps an adolescent boy develop positive gender-role characteristics; adolescent girls are more likely to form positive opinions of men and are better able to relate to them when parented by an involved father.

The bottom line is this: children are directly impacted by the involvement (or lack of involvement) of their fathers. Your children need you to help them be the best version of themselves that they can possibly be. *Social competence and relational competence can only be mastered when one has a healthy perspective of self.*

In our time in ministry and higher education, my husband and I have witnessed the aftermath left by both abusive and absent fathers. I've counseled teenage girls who were never taught to respect themselves and who made terrible decisions based on who wanted their bodies at the time. Many of them struggled with eating disorders. We've also mentored teenage boys who lacked both confidence and a strong sense of self because they lacked healthy male affection. These guys craved time with a stable male influence.

On the flip side, I can easily tell you which teens come from stable, loving homes. I can point out girls who were blessed with fathers who encouraged and empowered them. Their fathers taught them to respect their bodies and to not settle for attention from males who wouldn't. I can also tell you the boys who were raised

---

27. Oliker, "The Importance of Fathers."

Constantly Pursuing Effective Parenting

to celebrate their full range of emotions and to respect themselves and others.

Fathers, don't downplay the importance of your influence on your children. Your influence will help them grow to their fullest potential—and our society will be better off for it.

DEAL WITH IT

Read and View

1. "Marriage Benefits Children."[28]
2. Sawhill, "Are Children Raised with Absent Fathers Worse Off?"[29]
3. "Stubborn Child: Total Transformation Testimonials."[30]

Think It Through

1. How does your own experience with marriage influence your desires for your children as they grow to maturity?
2. What is the relationship between discipline and respect?
   - Do you discipline children differently than your parents disciplined you?
   - In what specific ways does your style of discipline differ from what you experienced as a child?
3. What changed in Jessie's environment in the video "Stubborn Child: Total Transformation Testimonials"?

Pray It Through

1. If you have "missed the mark" (sinned) as a parent, seek God's forgiveness and wisdom to know how to become a more effective father.
2. Pray with your children, asking God to help you be the best father in the world.
3. Ask God to increase your awareness of the relational competence of your children.

---

28. https://firstthings.org/marriage-benefits-children.
29. https://www.brookings.edu/opinions/are-children-raised-with-absent-fathers-worse-off/.
30. YouTube video: https://www.youtube.com/watch?v=0BCS3Q1lDjY.

Constantly Pursuing Effective Parenting

4. Pray specifically for his divine intervention in parenting situations that have left you feeling angry and defeated.

Act on It

1. View with your wife Tolpin and Tolpin, "How to Raise Kids to Respect Their Parents."[31]

   - Stop the video as needed in order to discuss with her the points you each find interesting.
   - Would your parents have benefitted from this video? If so, in what ways?

2. If you have one or more children, share with each of them privately how your parents disciplined you. If possible, share this personal history with their mother present, so she can add her own history with parental discipline.

3. If applicable and appropriate to your situation, apologize to your children for reacting in anger to their behavior.

4. Explain to your wife how this chapter has impacted you.

---

31. YouTube video: https://www.youtube.com/watch?v=r41tVNIZTZU.

7

Constantly Seducing

"There's always truth in seduction. That's why it works."
Zoe Archer[1]

INTRODUCTION

Welcome to the chapter you have been waiting[2] to read. The word *seduction* is without question a seductive, attention-capturing word! But what exactly is seductive? Perhaps it is the provocative fragrance of scented oils and scattered rose petals, or the flickering glow of candles, or that passionate, come-hither look in your wife's eyes. These are some of the images and memories indelibly linked by movies, or our own history, to the word *seduction*.

The entertainment industry unfortunately portrays seduction as an outside-of-marriage adventure. Though frequently lauded, seduction is pictured as something manipulative and life-altering.

---

1. Taken from http://www.wiseoldsayings.com/seduction-quotes/.

2. Or not waiting: you may have started reading here, just to see if the book was "worth the purchase price!"

Constantly Seducing

Movies[3] and non-Christian novels often depict wives being seduced, but not by their husbands. The thought of a married couple using seductive "moves" to enhance their marriage seems odd, if not outright repulsive, to those who applaud adultery.

This marriage-has-nothing-to-do-with-it mindset is both pervasive and regrettable. And who makes these "rules" anyway? Certainly not Bible-believing Christian men! The Song of Songs, about three thousand years old, is loaded with seductive, even graphic, chatter between married lovers.[4] While most pastors have never preached a sermon series from that book, they will freely recommend it during the last premarital counseling session.

This chapter first highlights the overall goal of constantly seducing: winning again her heart and body (note the sequence). It then examines five key avenues of a Christian husband's seduction:

- Gentleness is seductive,
- Cleanliness is seductive,
- Romance is seductive,
- Exclusiveness is seductive,
- Fitness-strength is seductive.

These avenues of seduction, with the exception of romance, might seem unexpected. All five are useful, however, for the man devoted to constantly pursuing his beloved. I encourage you to read each section with an open mind, and with your wife *in* mind.

THE GOAL: WINNING HER HEART AND BODY—AGAIN

Before exploring the interesting details, let's briefly consider the big picture of marital seduction. As suggested above, the primary objective of your seductive "moves" must be your wife's heart. Her

---

3. For example, the 1993 movie *Indecent Proposal*, starring Robert Redford, Demi Moore, and Woody Harrolson.
4. Especially the passion-filled verses in chapter 7.

body willingly follows her heart; *rarely* does it work the other way around. In fact, her heart *is* the heart of the matter in a satisfying lifetime of sexual enjoyment and passion.

I argue in this chapter that seduction should, in part, characterize a Christian husband's constant pursuit of his wife. Seduction is, in my view, totally appropriate for married Christian couples—with no gender discrimination! Yes, wives often enjoy flirting with, teasing, and seducing their husbands. Generally, however, their husbands are the pursuers, seeking to seduce (once again) their delightful wives.

Here's the amazing reality for the constantly seducing husband: the process *never* gets old, *never* becomes boring.[5] Fresh creativity, an active imagination, and a passionate desire to give pleasure all empower this great adventure! The husband who complains that sex has become boring unwittingly incriminates himself; through his complaints, he acknowledges that he is either uncreatively dull or selfishly lazy . . . or both. As his wife changes and grows,[6] so his pursuit must change, adapt, and grow. Therapist Logan Levkoff[7] put the matter directly:

> OK guys, stop all your whining and complaining for a second and listen up: If you want more sex from your wives, you have to grow up and recognize that people change, relationships change, and your sex life doesn't stay the same.

Boring sex is a self-inflicted, marriage-threatening malady. "Constantly seducing" is the life-sustaining (and marriage-extending) cure. Embrace the cure: seek to win her heart and her body—again!

As described in the following five sections, almost everything a husband does (and *is*) either contributes to or diminishes his appeal to his wife. Only a fool would constantly pursue a single woman's heart (and, eventually, her body), only to terminate his

---

5. After more than 47 years of pursuit, I am still learning, still amazed, still pursuing, and still *never* bored!

6. See chapter 3: "Constantly Pursuing the Moving Target."

7. Levkoff, "Fox on Sex: 5 Ways." Logan is a female.

Constantly Seducing

pursuit at their wedding altar. A wise and patient lover will *continue* to pursue, to seduce, to treasure his treasure for decades of delightful intimacy and fulfillment.

GENTLENESS IS SEDUCTIVE

Let's start the rest of this chapter right by focusing on the most seductive thing a man can do: pursue her *gently*. Gentle pursuit requires loving *tenderly* and speaking *softly*. Sir, it is the gentleness of your voice, not the power of your loins, that your wife finds most seductive. Loving phrases, whispered passion, stories of real or imagined pursuit: these are foundational to your ongoing gentle seduction of your wife. Lasting marital satisfaction begins here.

Unlike the now-archaic term *gentleman*,[8] the word *gentle* remains timeless and relevant. A *gentle* man possesses a magical key[9] to his wife's heart! Perhaps he saw gentleness modeled by his father or other male hero. In any case, his gentleness is powerfully seductive. Like the biblical term *meekness*, the word *gentleness* speaks of strength under control: well-mannered power. This description of restrained masculinity forms the bedrock of marital bliss. Other avenues of marital seduction pale by comparison.

A husband's persistent gentleness assures his wife that she is *safe*: his passion will bless her, never harm her. His gentle touch promises that nothing will happen to her that she doesn't want to happen! His sensitivity to her needs assures his wife that their marital bed comfortably sleeps two. Strength under control: *that*, sir, is seductive. Vikki Claflin[10] spoke for most wives: "We want to feel loved, appreciated, noticed, and desirable, even when we're not naked. If you can do that, we'll rock your world on a regular basis."

---

8 As a descriptor of a given individual, this term is now almost never used except in the context of military officers greeting each other, the gentle "Ladies and gentlemen" greeting, and the race announcer's "Gentlemen, start your engines."

9. Perhaps I should say "secret key," given how pervasive domestic violence currently is in US society.

10. Claflin, "A Lesson for the Menfolk."

Sir, you may have mistakenly embraced a twisted view of masculinity, one that reflects the content of violent or pornographic movies. The perverted imaginations of secular movie makers have *nothing* to do with real life—Conan the Barbarian is *not* the masculine ideal, and Christian sexuality comes in only one "shade": pure white![11] Yes, you can choose to behave crudely around your wife. Yes, you can bombard her with strange demands and selfish desires. Doing so, however, is stupid and relationally perilous.

Time for a reality check, sir. You will get less, not more, of what you *really* want without the aid of seductive gentleness. Scripture clearly teaches that we reap what we sow. For example, Galatians 6:7 states, *"Do not be deceived: God is not mocked, for whatever one sows, that will he also reap."* Sow crude behavior and weird, selfish demands in the bedroom and reap a lifetime of "Not tonight, dear, I still have a terrible headache."[12]

CLEANLINESS IS SEDUCTIVE

Many people believe that the Bible actually states . . . somewhere . . . "cleanliness is next to godliness."[13] Cleanliness is not next to godliness, but it definitely will help you get next to your wife! I have often seen my wife's I've-got-to-get-out-of-here response to my sweaty gym clothes as I hang them in the laundry room.[14] In fact, she recently admitted that the pervasive odor emanating from those clothes often motivates her to (quickly) start another load of laundry! No hugs, no kisses, no passionate embrace until the magic

   11. *Pure* white, like the gown adorning a chaste virgin on her wedding day.

   12. This generalization in no way is intended to demean women who frequently struggle with migraine headaches.

   13. Notice the lack of italics in this non-biblical statement. See https://www.gotquestions.org/cleanliness-next-godliness.html for background information about this error in biblical understanding.

   14. As an aside, it never ceases to amaze me how long it takes me to clean up after myself: dirty clothes carried to the laundry room, dirty dishes washed in the sink, used tools returned to their proper storage. My wife *always* appreciates the fact that she does not need to "pick up after me." She is not my house cleaner!

Constantly Seducing

of a soapy shower cleanses the sweat-soaked flesh. Hugs, kisses, and lingering embraces are freely welcomed thereafter. She loves the fact that I embrace cardiovascular exercise; she also remains highly motivated to *avoid* my embrace immediately thereafter!

Speaking of hugs, consider carefully this amazing observation from Ivan Verr:[15]

> Did you know that hugging a woman for at least 30 seconds a day makes her body release an hormone called oxytocin which will make her feel loved and "in the mood" for love? Well, now you know. . . . Just hug your wife every day for at least 30 seconds, and see what happens. Don't do anything else, and do not escalate to sex. . . . She will start feeling like you genuinely care about her and that you're not just trying to get her to bed. This is the starting point to build that unconditional sexual connection that couples in happy marriages have.

What's the application? Get clean—body, breath, hair, fingernails—and get busy hugging. Warm and wonderful things await a clean, gentle hugger!

So, cleanliness is not next to godliness, but it *is* foundational to satisfying, God-exalting sex. Albert Mohler[16] offered great perspective here: "Put most bluntly, I believe that God means for a man to be civilized, directed, and stimulated toward marital faithfulness by the fact that his wife will freely give herself to him sexually." He then added a terms-and-conditions-apply proviso to this happy outcome: "*only* when he presents himself as worthy of her attention and desire."[17] Applying Mohler's advice to this section, her freely-give-herself response in the bedroom depends in large measure on his freely-wash-his-armpits initiative . . . in the shower!

Husbands and wives need to grow to the point they can be honest with each other about cleanliness, without risk of offense. One blogger observed,

---

15. Verr, "How to Seduce Your Wife Again."
16. Mohler, "The Seduction of Pornography." (For fastest internet search, omit the author's last name.)
17. Emphasis added.

I'm not wounded by my wife asking, "When did you shower last?," or by her saying "Do you mind if I take a shower first?" She's just looking to have the best possible experience, for both of us.[18]

Cleanliness is seductive, a process that works both directions, but more often than not in the direction of the Christian husband longing to bless his wife with a clean lover and to *be* blessed in return.

ROMANCE IS SEDUCTIVE

Intentionally seductive, romantic acts help to create an atmosphere of pursuit and persuasion. A romantic man is creative and focused; his intentions are clear, and his money backs those intensions. A candlelit dinner, fragrant roses, soft music gently playing, and later (if all proceeds as planned) lingering kisses and passionate embraces: all of these expressions of romance are aimed at encouraging his wife to welcome his additional advances.

Romance plays such a major role in our popular culture because (1) women love it, and (2) men love women. If you doubt part 1 of this two-part explanation, consider these fascinating facts[19] about the romance-novel industry:

- The romance fiction industry is worth just over one billion dollars a year;
- Women compose a whopping 84% of all romance-novel readers;
- The largest segment (41%) of romance-novel readers are between 30 and 54 years old;
- Regular romance-novel buyers tend to be voracious readers: 46 percent of those consumers read at least one book per week.

---

18. Dee, "Being Clean for Sex."
19. For additional details, see Peterson, "Here Is What You Need to Know."

Constantly Seducing

My guess is that many romance-novel readers are romance-*starved* Christian wives. They are married to men—probably good men—who are sadly clueless about the hunger women feel for romance. Perhaps these guys once grasped the importance of romance, back when they were courting, but allowed it to slide off of their marriage-relationship radar. Sir, if your wife is spending 15% of the family's income on romance novels (even the Christian kind), it is time for a romance-is-seductive reality check.

What is so romantic about romance? Romantic acts target her heart and (if all goes well) seduce her mind. And the words matter! They matter in romance novels, and they matter in Solomon's Song of Songs. A Song-of-Songs-type man knows the power of words to win . . . again . . . his wife's heart and mind.[20] In this context, William Drake[21] offered a powerful observation about romance and seduction:

> Seduction is not about strategy . . . it's more about knowing your partner and then catching them by surprise, reminding them of the attraction that exists and has always existed between you two. Seduction of your spouse is a reminder that the love you have together is still red-hot and that you are willing to chase her, as always, being the dashing romantic you are.

The "dashing romantic"—did you catch that phrase in the quote above? Romantic men *romance* the women they love. They do this (generally) through some of the same actions that won her in the first place! We call it *courtship* and it is characterized by:

- Letting her know she is your top priority
- Walking together hand in hand, or with your hand on her waist or shoulder
- Singing love songs to her
- Investing time and money in her and in her pleasure
- Opening the car door for her

---

20. A man who wins his wife's heart and mind is, by definition, a winner!
21. Drake, "How to Seduce Your Wife."

- Writing love letters to her even though she hasn't traveled anywhere
- Surprising her with texts on her phone and flowers on her table
- Doing the unexpected, but not the unplanned[22]

Here I reluctantly confess my failure. I don't always get this romance-is-seductive business right, but when I do . . . well . . . I highly recommend the effort!

During his sermon on the mount, Jesus confronted his listeners with his new standard of behavior: *"whatever you wish that others would do to you, do also to them"* (Matt 7:12). When honestly applied to a man's heart and behavior, this verse emphasizes his willingness to give, not take. Ivan Verr phrased this principle pointedly: "Giving her pleasure has to become your pleasure. . . . This is the mindset that will get you far when seducing your wife."[23] Pleasure is *most* pleasurable when shared.

Sir, this section has pushed you to focus on *her* pleasure, not your own. A healthy woman saturated with romantic, seductive acts that are motivated by love and sincere desire will respond passionately, eager to give back. Stay focused on her pleasure and joy, then trust the process of romantic seduction to leave you *both* thoroughly satisfied.

EXCLUSIVENESS IS SEDUCTIVE

Almost every married man has, at least once in his life, publicly responded to questions like these:

> Do you, ___ [groom's name], take ___ [bride's name] to be your wedded wife, to live together in holy matrimony? Do you promise to love her, comfort her, honor and keep her for better or worse, for richer or poorer, in sickness

---

22. Many women love it when they discover that their husbands are making romantic, seductive plans for them!

23. Verr, "How to Seduce."

Constantly Seducing

and health, and *forsaking all others*, be faithful only to her, for as long as you both shall live?"[24]

If you are still not sure, "I do" is the correct answer to these edgy, no-wiggle-room questions. I assume you answered correctly. Even if you were nervous and soft spoken, God heard your answer. Family and friends heard your answer. And ___ [bride's name] heard your answer. The phrase "I do" uttered in this context becomes a life-altering pair of words!

Unfriendly Forsake-Ment

Marriage vows are more than just for-better-or-worse commitments. They are vows of *exclusive* faithfulness, vows of comprehensive forsake-ment, vows that the marital bed sleeps two—*only* two. If you truly kept that vow, sir, you forsook *all* others. Obviously "others" included old girlfriends. "Others" must also include emotion-stained memorabilia. Old emails: forsaken and deleted. Old, no-longer-memorized phone numbers: forsaken and erased. Social media "friend" connections: forsaken and unfriended. A typical marriage vow, in fact, demands an *un*friend-ly approach to the past, and a *very* friendly (exclusive) approach to the future with only ___ [bride's name].

Why Exclusiveness Is Seductive

Exclusiveness is seductive because it locks jealousy out of the house. Blessed is the wife who is certain that she is her husband's only source of joy and release. She is free to be the uninhibited husband-pleasing lover she longs to be. In fact, his imagination has only one channel, and it is labeled "___ [bride's name]"! Forsake-ment empowers exclusiveness; it must be ruthless, comprehensive, and executed long before the wedding day.

Exclusiveness is seductive, sir, because your imagination is focused on only one woman. In a biblical marriage, you *cannot*

---

24. Adapted from "Traditional 'I Do' Vows." Emphasis added.

have a digital hottie waiting nearby in your computer. Stated bluntly, you cannot forsake "all others" and continue to ingest pornographic images or videos. Doing so will break your vow, threaten your marriage, and humiliate your wife. She can never be certain if you are thinking of her or another woman (real or digital) during foreplay and sex.

Exclusiveness is seductive because your wife is safe within your bedroom's no-competition zone. Logan Levkoff observed that "women want to feel connected . . . in ways that don't always involve sex."[25] Exclusiveness guarantees that connection is totally successful.

So, ___ [bride's name] dreams of surrendering her body to a porn-free, one-woman man. Albert Mohler forcefully argued that "pornography is a slander against the goodness of God's creation." He then warned,

> The deliberate use of pornography is nothing less than the willful invitation of illicit lovers and objectified sex objects and forbidden knowledge into a man's heart, mind, and soul. The damage to the man's heart is beyond measure, and the cost in human misery will only be made clear on the Day of Judgment.[26]

Sir, you made the "I do" vow . . . *keep your vow!* Find joy and delight in the seductive power of your exclusive focus on ___ [bride's name]. Tell her often and show her consistently that she is the only one for you, that you have forsaken "all others" for the passionate joy of being with her.

FITNESS-STRENGTH IS SEDUCTIVE

"All other things being equal": that phrase is essential when comparing two states or conditions or (as discussed in this section) bodies! Whatever those "other things" might be, the comparison

---

25. Levkoff, "Fox on Sex: 5 Ways."
26. Mohler, "The Seduction." (For fastest internet search, use "The Seduction of Pornography.")

Constantly Seducing

that follows is illumined by this encompassing phrase. Moving from abstract-ness to specific-ness, let's consider ___ [bride's name]'s response to *your* body! Picture it: she's looking you up and down as you emerge from the shower. Now, to maximize the illustration's impact, let's imagine two dramatically distinct versions of your body:

1. Version 1 is 65 pounds over your goal weight, boasting biceps that haven't produced a push up in six years. Your bulging gut is larger than your chest, and a single flight of stairs leaves you breathless and dizzy.

2. Version 2 is, in a single word, buff! Strong and toned, your muscles automatically flex as you dry yourself. Your stomach boasts a visible six-pack, and your legs are beautifully chiseled from training for that upcoming 10K race.

Now, let's ask ___ [bride's name] to compare these two versions of you! Same husband, same character, same love, same devotion, and same intellect. Which will she choose? Well, "all other things being equal," she probably will choose Version 2. Why? Fitness and strength are far more seductive than flab and weakness. True, ___ [bride's name] may never state this aloud (or even allow herself to think it): such is the vision-distorting power of love. But if she were actually given the choice . . . if love wasn't needed to filter out the flab . . . .

My "take away" from this little exercise is simple: you and I need to do what we need to do to empower Version 2.[27] I am not suggesting that you need to become an Olympic athlete or run a marathon next week. I *am* suggesting, sir, that you do need to do *something* daily to remain (or become)[28] easy on the eyes for ___ [bride's name]! Vivian Diller observed that we "can't stop the aging process, but there are things we can do to prolong the health and vitality of our faces and bodies so we remain attractive to our

---

27. Yes, the rhyming scheme in this sentence was intentional.

28. If you are unsure where to start, the readings at the end of this chapter and my recently published book, *Sweaty, Sore, Sometimes Hungry*, will prove useful.

mates."[29] Fitness and strength are seductive: "that's my story and I'm sticking to it!"

LISTEN TO THE LADY: CONVERSATION IS KEY

When I read the section "Romance is Seductive," I wanted to stand up and applaud Marvin on behalf of women everywhere. Romance takes more than a cheap thrill. What is portrayed to men in Hollywood films is a farce; women don't get turned on by cat-calls or comments about their body parts. Husband, it takes a lot more than your admiration for your wife's beauty to hold her attention and affection. What she *really* wants is time with you and your undivided attention.

Romance is not always expressed through roses and weekend getaways,[30] but it does need the power of intentional planning. Quality time together doesn't happen by accident or magically of its own accord. By quality time, I mean this: time the two of you aren't tending to the needs of your children or staring at your phone displays or the TV screen. Quality time is about quality conversation. It's when you and your wife are genuinely focused on one another and engaged in endearing conversation. It's about the *verbal* long before anything gets *physical*.

Many women enjoy meeting with their girlfriends for meaningful conversation. Your wife may be one of them, but she also desires that level of attentive sharing with *you*. There's a reason jokes exist about husbands who don't listen. When you have a conversation with your wife, eliminate all distractions. Don't try to listen to her while you're checking the score on your phone or watching the news. When you speak *to* her, make sustained eye contact *with* her.

I suggest you take this quick test to see how well you know your wife:

    29. Diller, "Maintaining Attraction." For additional details about the research that supports Diller's conclusion, see Diller, "Is Love Really Blind?"
    30. But don't overlook these, either! She still likes them.

Constantly Seducing

1. What did she do this week?
2. Did her week energize or exhaust her?
3. What are your wife's favorite hobbies?
4. What are her top priorities? What values does she hold most dear?
5. What goals has your wife set for the future? For herself? For your family?
6. Are you working together to achieve those goals?
7. Can you name your wife's three closest friends?
8. Can your wife answer these questions about you?

If the answer to any of these questions is a big blank, then guess what? You have a starting point for a conversation that will help you know your wife even better and a chance to let her know more of your heart. If you know the answers to all of these questions, then you have conversation topics for further exploration. Welcome to bonding with your wife. She longs to know that what is important to her is also important to you. That, Mr. Husband, is truly romantic!

So how do you get there? You get there by making a plan! When can you and your wife have quality time together, even if over a meal or an early cup of coffee at the kitchen table? How can you make this a weekly habit? Your interest in reserving time for the two of you will speak romantic volumes to her.

The old adage warns: "Failure to plan is planning to fail."[31] I strongly recommend that you plan accordingly.

---

31. Adapted from https://quoteinvestigator.com/2018/07/08/plan/.

DEAL WITH IT

READ AND VIEW

1. "80 Ways to Show Your Wife You Love Her."[32]
2. Diller, "Maintaining Attraction in Long-Term Relationships."[33]
3. Drake, "How to Seduce Your Wife and Be Romantic."[34]
4. Zhang, "How to Seduce Your Wife: Everyday Practical Tips."[35]

THINK IT THROUGH

1. What is your primary take-away from Zhang's article? What can you do differently in your efforts to constantly seduce your wife?
2. Are you comfortable with the term *seduction* in the context of Christian marriage? If not, can you think of another term that would communicate the same (or similar) idea?
3. What changes, if any, do you need to make in your appearance, self-care, and grooming? Be specific.

PRAY IT THROUGH

1. Ask the Lord to sensitize you to your wife's need to be desired, pursued, and treasured.
2. Repent for any lingering involvement with pornography. Confess your sins and seek God's forgiveness.
3. Pray for wisdom regarding your future use of computers and other potential access points to pornographic images.

---

32. https://www.familylifeshare.com/how-to-show-your-wife-you-love-her/.
33. https://www.psychologytoday.com/us/blog/face-it/201205/maintaining-attraction-in-long-term-relationships.
34. https://www.betterhelp.com/advice/marriage/how-to-seduce-your-wife-and-be-romantic/.
35. https://www.familylifeshare.com/how-to-seduce-your-wife/.

Constantly Seducing

4. Search your heart honestly before the Lord regarding any relationship or friendship that could in *any* way negatively impact your wedding vow and commitment to remain a one-woman man.

Act on It

1. Read to your wife: Mohler, "The Seduction of Pornography and the Integrity of Christian Marriage, Part 2."[36]

   - Invite her to comment or question as you read.

   - Commit in her presence to becoming or remaining accountable to her and to God for what you read and view in the future.

2. Read to your wife the list of eight actions listed in this chapter (107–108) typically associated with courtship. Ask her to add to that list actions that she views as romantic-seductive gestures (e.g., carrying a heavy bag for her, surprising her with a carefully chosen card). Take careful note of her response.

3. Delete or destroy any existing communication or potential for communication with all former girlfriends. Then describe to your wife how that process makes you feel.

4. Adopt and consistently implement *The Pence Rule*.[37] Applications of *The Pence Rule* include:

   - Never text or email a woman without copying (cc-ing) the message to your wife.

   - Never meet with a woman, in public or in private, without another person—preferably your wife—present during the entire meeting.

---

36. https://www.christianpost.com/news/the-seduction-of-pornography-and-the-integrity-of-christian-marriage-part-2.html.

37. See Garbarino, "If Men Don't Want to Get Kavanaughed." Note that *The Pence Rule* was originally labeled *The Billy Graham Rule*. I commend the courage and wisdom of both men.

5. Implement a specific, multi-point plan to become (or remain) physically attractive to your wife.
6. Explain to your wife how this chapter has impacted you.

8

Pursuing in Pain

"Endurance is not just the ability to bear a hard thing, but to turn it into glory."

WILLIAM BARCLAY[1]

INTRODUCTION

This final chapter was a painful writing experience, one I wanted to terminate before reaching the last sentence. Such is the nature of pain, whether it is physical or mental-emotional! Pain is, in fact, the consistent point of reference in this chapter's five main topics. Each topic addresses a unique relational challenge. Some challenges are more painful than others, as will become obvious throughout this chapter.

---

1. Taken from https://www.brainyquote.com/quotes/william_barclay_186928.

Two Painful Principles

I begin this push to the last sentence by briefly highlighting two aspects of pain I advanced in an earlier book.[2] First, *pain is a given in life*. Pain dominates our entrance[3] and will likely dominate our exit. A Christian husband knows that his Lord was prophetically labeled *"a man of sorrows"* (Isa 53:3) because pain played a dominant role in his life and death. Thus, to embrace "sorrows" (aka *pain*) in the context of the Christian life is one of the most spiritual things a man can do. Sir, do not allow pain to defeat you. Resist its temptation to stop, turn around, or take a short cut.

Second, *pain and joy are comfortable companions*. Until I developed cancer in 2014, I had always assumed that these were mutually exclusive human experiences. Now I know better. The deepest, most treasured joy we can ever know is sometimes (perhaps always) found in life's most painful situations. Pain is a stripper! It strips away our ego, arrogance, and pride. It leaves us naked, helpless, and desperate: the three prerequisite conditions for God's full intervention in our lives. And his intervention (his touch, his presence) *always* births joy in our souls.

Cross-Taking Pain

Our tears can be triggered by either pain or joy; occasionally they are triggered by both experiences. Ultimately, the source—the primary "trigger"—does not matter. What matters is becoming more like the Master: tender, loving, seeking, forgiving. This is *the* goal of our cross-taking[4] endurance. The circumstances surrounding our marital relationships (some joyful, others painful) contribute

---

2. My book, *Sweaty, Sore, Sometimes Hungry*, was published by Resource Publications, an imprint of Wipf and Stock Publishers.

3. Mothers call it *labor*; newborns would call it *horrific, face-smashing contortion* if they could stop crying long enough.

4. *"If anyone would come after me, let him deny himself and take up his cross daily and follow me"* (Luke 9:23).

uniquely to the spiritual summons to take up our cross and follow our Lord as a husband, father, and man of God.

The topics of painful pursuit addressed in this chapter are:

- Pursuing consistently
- Pursuing uphill
- Pursuing a wounded heart
- Pursuing an unfaithful wife
- Pursuing peace with your former wife

PURSUING CONSISTENTLY

Consistency is a difficult word; some people distain it because consistency suggests both unrelenting effort and goal-focused behavior. They would rather embrace the delusional freedom of spontaneity, pursuing whatever feels good at the moment. Consider these widely divergent opinions about the contribution of consistency to our lives:[5]

- Consistency "is the hallmark of the unimaginative" (literary giant Oscar Wilde).
- Consistency is "contrary to nature, contrary to life. The only completely consistent people are the dead" (writer, philosopher Aldous Huxley).
- Success "is neither magical nor mysterious. Success is the natural consequence of consistently applying basic fundamentals" (entrepreneur E. James Rohn).
- Consistency is a life-shaping force: "It's not what we do once in a while that shapes our lives. It's what we do consistently" (motivational speaker Tony Robbins).

---

5. Taken from https://www.goodreads.com/quotes/tag/consistency.

Embracing a Positive View of Consistency

Among those quoted above, who is right? Obviously, I believe in the transforming power of consistency when applied to the tasks, the things, and the people I value most. I learned to value consistency on the football practice field by repeating the same drill, in the same stance, week after week, until it became second nature. I learned to value it in Air Force basic training, discovering how to march as part of a large group, with a consistent gait, at a consistent cadence. Those who value freedom and spontaneity over consistency may have flashes of creativity.[6] Yet in the family, *inconsistent* husbands will eventually shatter trust and disappoint those nearest to them.

What does Scripture say about consistency? James 1:3–4 states, *"for you know that the testing of your faith produces steadfastness. And let steadfastness have its full effect, that you may be perfect and complete, lacking in nothing."* Similarly, Paul admonished the Corinthians to *"be steadfast, immovable, always abounding in the work of the Lord, knowing that in the Lord your labor is not in vain"* (1 Cor 15:58). The biblical standard of living is summarized well in that Pauline phrase, *"steadfast, immovable"*: both terms are synonyms of the word *consistent*. These verses call a Christian husband to embrace steadfastness: staying highly focused in his pursuit of the treasure he already holds.

Motivational speaker Roy T. Bennet lauded consistency, arguing it is "the true foundation of trust."[7] He then linked consistency to character: "Either keep your promises or do not make them." Sir, your wife will probably welcome your promises to change an irritating behavior or obnoxious habit. It is your *consistent effort*, however, that will cause her to trust you more tomorrow than she did yesterday.

Pursuing your wife consistently is, without question, often tiring and thrill-less. Yet consistency empowers you to build a growing, one-flesh covenant-based lifetime relationship. And that

---

6. People such as artists and writers like Wilde and Huxley are included.

7. Taken from https://www.goodreads.com/quotes/7724637-consistency-is-the-true-foundation-of-trust-either-keep-your.

relationship is characterized by ever-deepening trust in each other and in the Lord of your marriage.

Striving for Consistent Effort, Not Perfection

It's time for some good news about pursuing consistently. Whether we use the term *consistently* or the closely related biblical term *steadfastly*, emphasis in this chapter is fixed on the for-the-long-haul *effort*. Nothing in this chapter promotes nobody-qualifies-anyway *perfection*. Pursuing constantly is a commitment every husband can and should make. That never-ending pursuit yields trust, joy, contentment, and rapid spiritual growth.

Jesus called (and still calls) his disciples to follow him in a radical rearrangement of their priorities: a purpose-soaked decision to put him first. Those men followed him consistently; *all twelve*—even Judas—stayed with him through times of political danger and transfixing awe, times of extreme fatigue and joyful refreshing. He knew they were (and we are) incapable of lifetime perfection. In fact, he took advantage of his disciples' imperfections to instruct, correct, and confront: all recorded in the Gospels for our benefit.[8] And they gave him ample opportunity to correct them! Yet he never told them to go away because they were imperfect. He valued their costly leave-the-nets commitment to follow him. It was the consistency, not the perfection, of their devotion to him that allowed Christ to build a triumphant church that hell's strongest defenses cannot withstand.[9]

Manly *Lead-mility*

Sir, you probably already know that commitment to pursue your wife consistently is a costly one: fatigue and failures impact all of us as Christian husbands. We "blow it" regularly in moments of anger,

---

8. Thanks, guys!

9. *"I will build my church, and the gates of hell shall not prevail against it"* (Matt 16:18b).

self-pity, or frustration. We may even "slack up" and "throttle back" at times when we grow pursuit-weary. Courage, man! Neither your wife *nor* your Lord demand husbanding perfection. The goal is consistency of effort, and *every* Christian husband is capable of that!

Greg Gibson powerfully argued that Christian husbands, imperfect as they (we) are, must man up: "You are the only one that can make her feel loved, cherished, pursued, and valued. It's all you. There's no one else. Period."[10] And what does she really want? She wants a *hybrid* man: a guy possessing quiet strength and *lead*ership skills while also displaying hu*mility*: willing to admit mistakes, to accept responsibility for his blunders, and to seek forgiveness for both. This hybrid man needs a hybrid term to describe him: she wants a *lead-mility* husband:

- A strong leader capable of standing on his own two feet: dependable and committed to leading his family well as the best representative of Jesus he can be;
- A humble husband (and father), willing to apologize, seek forgiveness, and confess his limitations.

Be that man, sir: be her one and only *lead-mility* lover!

PURSUING "UPHILL"

"Uphill" is always more challenging than "level ground" or "downhill." Yes, the word is shorter, but suggests no shortcuts, no rest, no easy places in a walk or run. "Uphill" may not be the preferred path, but it is the path that some men must take in life. This section explains why.

Running the Eland—Sacrificially

One of the most amazing videos I have ever watched recorded a Sān (Bushman) hunter running down—on foot—a one-ton Eland bull.[11]

---

10. Gibson, "Pursuing Your Wife."
11. Eland are the largest of the antelope family, thriving in arid terrain

Pursuing in Pain

The man survived the chase, the Eland didn't. What I had assumed was impossible obviously is possible, but only if the hunter constantly and intelligently pursues his quarry. The pain of that eight-hour chase must have been excruciating for the man; it obviously was for the exhausted Eland. Yet the meat that animal yielded likely fed his entire clan for a month or more. A staggering sacrifice of energy produced an amazing blessing for all as the clan welcomed home the successful, exhausted hunters.

Some long-distance runs, like that of the hunter, are sacrificial, motivated by a greater good. Greg Smalley[12] pictured the act of husbanding as a sacrificial effort:

> What does that sacrifice look like in our busy, day-to-day world? It's simply taking something that we value—time, money, resources, etc.—and giving it up for someone we see as *more* valuable. It communicates to our spouse that he or she truly means more to us than anything on earth.

Pursuing consistently does not require exceptional speed, but it does demand consistent *effort*. Obviously, the Eland-hunt metaphor eventually breaks down when applied to marriage: a loving husband's goal is *not* a totally exhausted, defenseless wife! Still, that image of the runner pursuing a prize of great value is a beautiful picture of Christian husbanding. It poignantly illustrates Smalley's insights (quoted above) regarding sacrificial marriage. She is worth the effort, the sacrifice, the moments of pain, and the occasional forfeit of personal freedom.

Those who pursue consistently sometimes risk "running on empty." Sir, your self-care is vital in a decades-long thriving marriage. In all your pursuing, remember to "fill up" regularly:

---

throughout southern Africa. That video was, as I recall, much longer (with less dramatic embellishment) than the BBC Earth production narrated by Richard Attenborough, "Human Mammal, Human Hunter." (See Attenborough in the Bibliography. The hunters in that video killed a Greater Kudu bull, the second-largest species of antelope.) I have no idea how either video was filmed; I cannot imagine a cameraman on foot keeping up with the hunter (and the hunted).

12. Smalley, "How to Pursue." Emphasis on the word *more* is in the original.

- Fill up on God through prayer, Scripture reading, and worship.
- Fill up on fellowship with friends and fellow believers.
- Fill up on the achievement of meaningful goals.
- Fill up on the joy and laughter children create in the home.
- And, of course, fill up on your responsive, warm, loving, passionate wife.

A Bushman is unable to pursue for hours if totally depleted. Similarly, marathon runners consume large quantities of calories and water during that twenty-six miles of self-inflicted pain. Constantly pursuing your wife does not demand perpetual neglect of yourself. Your physical, mental, and spiritual health really do matter in this lifetime "marathon" called Christian marriage.

Running Without a Role Model

Running uphill is far more exhausting than running on level ground. Similarly, pursuing your wife when you have never seen pursuit done . . . at least not well . . . can become emotionally draining. Some men reading this chapter know well the pain of that uphill run. Their fathers were not present[13] when they were growing. Other men had fathers who were ineffectively present: either abusive or simply clueless about pursuit.[14] Still other men remember that their fathers were too interested in work, money, or other women to model effective wife pursuit. In any case, constant, consistent pursuit seems unnatural for some men; at best, it is not instinctive.[15] This book may, for them, read more like a work of fiction than a non-fiction handbook for husbands.

13. Functionally or physically. Review the section titled "Negotiating Conflict" in chapter 3.

14. Or they simply lacked the desire to pursue; perhaps those men never saw the benefit in *their* parents' marriages.

15. Review the description of Son Sammy in the subsection titled, "The Power of Modeling" in chapter 6.

Pursuing in Pain

Trying to figure out this wife-pursuit business without childhood "training" is comparable to running a long-distance race on a course that goes only uphill. Role models make manageable so many challenges in life. A given new husband—let's call him Tim—will almost instinctively pursue the treasure he holds if his father modeled well his own pursuit of Tim's mother. Tim and his new bride are richly blessed by his father's commitment to faithful, consistent pursuit. His father's role modeling constitutes a next-generation blessing, an inheritance worth far more than a life insurance policy.

If, sir, you were raised without benefit of a constantly pursuing role model, many topics in this book will not resonate instinctively. Words like *tenderness*, *gentleness*, and *persistence* in the context of marriage may still read a bit like a foreign language. And their lived-out "pronunciation" in daily life may feel awkward on your "tongue." For you, I offer two deeply held convictions as sources of encouragement:

- You *can* learn to speak this language fluently, even if it is not your "mother tongue."

- Your children *will* adopt the language of gentle, tender pursuit as their "heart" language simply by watching you as you constantly, consistently (even if awkwardly, at first) pursue their mother.

Running uphill for a lifetime of faithful pursuit: unquestionably, this is at times an exhausting test of endurance. It is *also* the greatest blessing you can bestow on your children. Accept the test! Don't remain trapped in marital mediocrity because your childhood environment was not ideal. Become the positive role model your father (for whatever reason) was not for you. *Run uphill*, if need be, sir, *so your children can run on level ground* in their own pursuit . . . in their own marriages. Be their role model. Show them how it is done!

PURSUING A WOUNDED HEART

"We all stumble in many ways. Anyone who is never at fault in what they say is perfect, able to keep their whole body in check" (Jas 3:2, NIV). I am not sure if the apostle James had husbands in mind when he wrote this verse, but application to Christian husbands is certainly easy. We stumble, mess up, and offend with some regularity. And when trust is shattered through our offense, we must embrace the challenge of pursuing a wounded heart. This section explores that challenge, using addiction to pornography as an example of a heart-wounding offense.

Pursuing Forgiveness and Healing

Quickly review the section titled "Exclusiveness Is Seductive" in chapter 7. As you do, imagine a Christian husband named Matt[16] who has just finished reading that section. He is suddenly distressed, gripped by deep sorrow and stinging regret because of his unresolved addiction to pornography. Yes, he has shut it down at times, with great effort. He knows, though, that the stronghold of porn remains alive and well within him: it is an unrelenting source of temptation. Working through the "Deal with It" section at the end of chapter 7, he senses the Holy Spirit strongly confronting and convicting him about this addiction.

This convicting work of the Spirit comes at a crisis moment in Matt's life. His wife, Dianne, has already been wounded by his defensive-deceptive behavior. She has often seen him quickly close his notebook computer when he was not expecting her near. His integrity-damaging denials have left a lingering odor of dishonesty in their home. Even worse, one day when Matt was working in the yard, Dianne saw a horrible pornographic image on his cell phone when she reached to answer it. His fanciful high-tech explanation for what she had seen was irrational and pathetic—and they both knew it!

---

16. With apology to all Christian husbands named Matt who do not consume porn.

Pursuing in Pain

Matt is now miserable, and Dianne is filled with painful doubts about her once-trusted husband. Pornography and its bodyguard, "deception," can easily erode the foundation of a Christian marriage. Dianne now struggles with self-doubt about her desirability to Matt, mixed with jealously for the nameless women who arouse her husband's passions. She feels a raw, conflicted mix of attraction and revulsion when Matt touches her. Is he still *truly* alone with her in their bedroom or is he mentally in a cheap motel room watching others engage in degrading sex acts? Is Matt still her trusted lover, or just a lust-filled voyeur?

Sin contaminates everything it touches. When it infects a relationship built on trust, like Matt and Dianne's marriage, only radical surgery can drain its poison and cleanse the wound. This surgery requires brutally honest, ego-shrinking repentance. Nothing else works: not with Matt's wife and *certainly* not with Matt's Lord.

Repentance was John the Baptist's favorite sermon topic! He often proclaimed, *"Repent, for the kingdom of heaven is at hand"* (Matt 3:2).[17] And what did John tell those who responded to his message? On at least one occasion, he told them to *"bear fruits in keeping with repentance"* (Luke 3:8a). Big John boldly told it like it was! But what kind of *"fruits"* did he have in mind? Wayne Jackson[18] was convinced that John's deep-cutting-surgery approach to repentance went *far* beyond "mere regret." It invoked such a profound turning (turning = *"fruits"*) that all of life changed for the true repenter. Bearing *"fruits in keeping with repentance"*: that phrase summarizes Matt's only real hope for his marriage . . . and his soul. Matt must urgently start growing some fruit.

Pursuing Reconciliation and Restored Trust

What, exactly, should miserable Matt the repentant fruit grower do first? He must "come clean" to expel sin's poison: clean with

---

17. Jesus, John's relative, loved that sermon so much he made it his own primary message (Matt 4:17).

18. Jackson, "What Is the Fruit of Repentance?"

God and clean with Dianne. Confession of sin driven by the Spirit's deep work of conviction empowers lasting transformation. King David wrote his penitent Psalm 51 following his adulterous "fling" with Bathsheba. In that Psalm, he declared, *"the sacrifices of God are a broken spirit; a broken and contrite heart, O God, you will not despise"* (51:17). That three-thousand-year-old truth still births hope in the souls of truly repentant people.

The changes in a person's life that characterize true repentance "must correspond to the gravity and nature of the offense. Otherwise, there simply is no repentance."[19] This radical approach to sin and repentance must drive Matt to his knees. Both Dianne and God will question the quality of his *"fruits in keeping with repentance"* without his evident brokenness.

Being reconciled to God is a spiritual matter; Matt must prioritize that reconciliation. Being reconciled to Dianne is a relational matter he must also prioritize. Even with his wholehearted turning, however, full restoration of trust in Matt will, *at best*, likely take Dianne some time. Both of these reconciliation efforts, in my view,[20] should begin with written letters. Reb Bradley[21] has offered guys like Matt some excellent guidelines for writing a marriage-salvaging letter to their wounded wives. That letter must contain the same level of sin-confessing honesty that marked Matt's initial prayers for forgiveness. Both of his great loves— Christ Jesus and Dianne—deserve a written letter, in addition to his verbal confessions.

Matt must clearly communicate his unreserved commitment to turn from sin and acknowledge the damage his addiction has inflicted on Dianne and on their marriage. She may struggle to offer her wholehearted forgiveness. Once shattered, trust heals slowly. He should, nonetheless, immediately start tending those *"fruits."* They include:

---

19. Jackson.

20. I base my view on decades of observing firsthand in counseling sessions the power of hand-written letters to bring healing and restoration.

21. Bradley, "Guidelines for Writing a Letter."

Pursuing in Pain

- Deleting every source of pornography on his phone, computer, and other devices;
- Deleting his entire viewing history on each device;
- Accepting the restricted viewing options[22] available on every internet browser;[23]
- Investing in accountability software for all means of accessing the internet, especially his telephone. (By using Covenant Eyes software,[24] for example, Matt can select Dianne as one of his "covenant" partners; she will then receive weekly summaries of what Matt has viewed on his phone);
- Finding a face-to-face accountability partner or group. Matt must meet regularly with at least one man who will be brutally honest and will demand the same level of honesty from him;
- Signing up with one or more special ministry groups online to receive counsel, encouragement, and direction for recovering from pornography addiction.[25]

The pain and embarrassment Matt experiences during this life-altering process become the fertilizer for the *"fruits"* that demonstrate true repentance and *"godly grief"* (2 Cor 7:10). Dianne's wounded heart may heal in time, especially if his own is broken. Both Matt and Dianne need healing; though broken, he must lead the way in that process. He must strive to become ... again ... the

---

22. See, for example, Britec, "Easy Way to Block Adult Websites." Note that YouTube has an easy-to-set filter. Those struggling with the temptation of easily-accessed YouTube websites must set the filter *and leave it set!*

23. I did this years ago as a safeguard, knowing how seductive a single image can be. A single click on a Christ-and-wife-dishonoring website link, sir, can start you down a slippery slope you do not want to be on. You will fall. Avoid the slope by directing your computer to block the link. This step is relatively simple: it does not demand the skills of a computer specialist!

24. See Eldred, "5 Tips to Accountability" for details about Covenant Eyes.

25. See, for example, Be Broken Ministries described at https://2.bebroken.com/.

man she deeply respects and trusts, the man she will freely give herself to . . . again! This positive outcome must become Matt's daily prayer.

PURSUING AN UNFAITHFUL WIFE

This difficult-to-write section first examines Hosea's troubled marriage, which became a living illustration of God's pursuing love for the nation of Israel. It then challenges a betrayed husband to not allow marriage "killers" to terminate what his wife's betrayal has deeply wounded. The Word of God has much to say about embracing hope and restraint while reaching out to the one who broke her marriage vows.

Life Lessons from a Prophet

Hosea, the Old Testament prophet, must have initially concluded he had not distinctly heard the voice of the Lord. What he heard as his first directive from the Almighty was, *"Go, take to yourself a wife of whoredom and have children of whoredom, for the land commits great whoredom by forsaking the Lord"* (Hos 1:2b). The holy God of Israel told him, essentially, "Go marry a whore!" As this odd story unfolds, Hosea's broken heart, plus the attention-grabbing names[26] God gave to this couple's children became object lessons for God's rebellious nation. Calling their children in at dinner time must have made quite an impact on the neighbors. Welcome to the prophets' club, Hosea!

At some later point, an unnamed lover seduced Hosea's wife Gomer and took her away. God then directed Hosea to "buy" her back and bring her home again:

> And the Lord said to me, "Go again, love a woman who is loved by another man and is an adulteress, even as the

---

26. All three names were God given: Jezreel (Hos 1:4–5, predicting a future great punishment of God's idolatrous people), No Mercy (1:6), and Not My People (1:9).

Pursuing in Pain

Lord loves the children of Israel, though they turn to other gods and love cakes of raisins." (Hos 3:1)

Most Old Testament prophets did not have an easy or glamorous life; heartbroken Hosea dramatically illustrates this generalization. God directed Hosea to pursue his unfaithful wife: to go after her, find her, then buy her back at personal expense. Like his three children, the prophet's love life became a living sermon illustration. Through Hosea's troubled marriage, God illustrated his relentless, pursuing love for his spiritually adulterous people. My guess is that Hosea was simultaneously honored by God's call and grieved by his life-long prophetic assignment. So, what did he do? He obeyed God and pursued her . . . despite his pain! He found adulterous Gomer, paid off her sneaky, greedy lover, and took her home.

What can we learn from God's interaction with Hosea, and Hosea's interaction with Gomer? At least three key lessons emerge from this story:

1. God values marriage and marital faithfulness, just as he values spiritual faithfulness. Clearly, he did not command Hosea to marry Gomer as an evangelism strategy!

2. God *commanded* Hosea to love Gomer again: to not give up on her, to not abandon hope. That kind of selfless love is a choice, typically a painful one! It is never just a feeling.

3. God indirectly told Hosea (and all grieving husbands who know this man's pain) what to do by describing beautifully his approach to unfaithful Israel:

> *Therefore, behold, I will allure her,*
> *and bring her into the wilderness,*
> *and speak tenderly to her.*
> *And there I will give her her vineyards*
> *and make the Valley of Achor*[27] *a door of hope.*

---

27. *Achor* means trouble. When a marriage is severely damaged by adultery, hope embraces a God-centered future.

And there she shall answer as in the days of her youth,
as at the time when she came out of the land of Egypt. (Hos 2:14-15)

Allure[28] her, get away—*alone*—with her, speak tenderly to her, give her reason to believe she has a future with her husband again. These vivid insights into God's still-passionate heart for Israel suggest strategies for pursuing an unfaithful wife. They speak of gentleness and tenderness, not the anger—violent rage, at times—a betrayed husband naturally feels. *Anger* and *allure* both start with the letter "a," but they impact a fragile marriage in dramatically different ways. God was enraged by his spiritually unfaithful nation (see Hos 2:2-13). Yet his final response (and plea) to his own, quoted above, was saturated in undeserved kindness, unmerited patience, and the promise of ample provision for his frustrating wayward "wife."

Killers in Your House

Sir, you may be living out Hosea's pain daily: the husband of a wayward wife and the father of confused children. She may have violated her vow out of loneliness, isolation, revenge, or a hundred other "reasons" for cheating. Still, you love her and want your marriage to survive. What now? What is your next move?

Marriage counseling with a Christian therapist or counselor can be a great blessing, especially if both of you are open to seeking help. I strongly encourage you to locate such a professional and begin rebuilding your marriage. This *always* painful process will likely take considerable time; much needs to change in your marital relationship.[29] In fact, pursuing her through the knee-deep emotional sewage her affair has left in your house will almost certainly be the greatest test of courage you have ever faced. Your instincts are telling you to yell, belittle, insult, attack, and strike out to "even

---

28. *Allure* is a synonym for *seduce*. Review chapter 7 for ways to become "alluring" (seductive) to your wife.
29. Smalley, "Marital Infidelity."

the score." Your instincts are wrong! Her unfaithfulness has not (yet) destroyed your marriage, but your ego-driven reactions may.

Three marriage killers moved into your guest bedroom as soon as you learned of her unfaithfulness. Each is a potent enemy. In combination, they can ruthlessly destroy what you sacrificially built. They destroy marriages; in some cases, they provoke the actual murder of family members. This destruction occurs in thousands of homes weekly! Like a category 5 hurricane, these three can blow away everything but memories:

1. Pride: "I'm waiting for her to come begging for forgiveness on her knees: no knees, no forgiveness!"
2. Anger: "I'll fix them both; they're not going to get away with this!"
3. Despair: "I will never be able to trust her again; there is nothing I can do . . . this mess is hopeless!"

Obviously, God has a thing or two[30] to say about each of these in-residence assassins. His Word is powerful, capable of disarming and then evicting them:

1. Pride: *"If you do not forgive others their trespasses, neither will your Father forgive your trespasses"* (Matt 6:15).
2. Anger: *"Be angry and do not sin; do not let the sun go down on your anger, and give no opportunity to the devil"* (Eph 4:26–27).
3. Despair: *"May the God of hope fill you with all joy and peace in believing, so that by the power of the Holy Spirit you may abound in hope"* (Rom 15:13).

If you let these killers stay in your house, they *will* destroy your marriage—and likely you in the process. Sir, your marriage has taken a huge hit. Nothing in this section is intended to minimize that. But if she has not yet ended your marriage, hope remains . . . *if* you let it (hope) stay in that now unused bedroom.

---

30. Actually, far more than "a thing or two" about each of these killers fill the pages of God's Word. Here, only one representative passage of Scripture speaks to each killer.

Jesus gives life to the dead, frees the prisoners, and restores the brokenhearted. *He can heal your fragile marriage* and do the same for your tormented emotions. Do *not* allow these killers to execute what you pledged to nurture for a lifetime. Pursue . . . again!

PURSUING PEACE WITH YOUR FORMER WIFE

Divorce is a tragedy, no matter its motivation-justification or who initiates it. A survey of over 2000 heterosexual couples revealed that "women initiated nearly 70 percent of all divorces."[31] Husbands tend to be unfaithful in much larger numbers than wives, a fact that likely contributed to this research finding. The high incidence of physical and emotional abuse inflicted by angry, selfish men doubtless contributed to this finding.

I have no personal history with separation and divorce, nor with marital unfaithfulness and betrayal. I have, however, counseled with couples in conflict: some before divorce, others during and even after their divorces were finalized. As a counselor, I have felt the dark intensity of their conflict. No couple reaches the point of marital dissolution without times of intense conflict. And their conflict does not end with the thundering whack of the judge's gavel. What happens thereafter heavily (sometimes brutally) impacts the couple *and* their children . . . sometimes even *"to the third and fourth generation"* (Exod 34:7).[32]

Scriptural Reasons to Pursue Peace

Is a conflict-free divorce possible? No. Can former spouses part as something other than mortal enemies? Yes. Some former spouses even report they have become close friends. While that outcome continues to baffle me, I do not doubt that a relatively amicable divorce is possible. Divorce attorney Karen Covy advised, "If you want

---

31. LaBier, "Women Initiate Divorce."

32. See Exod 20:5, Num 14:18, and Deut 5:9 for additional references to this intriguing, ominous phrase.

your divorce to be amicable, you have to start by deciding that keeping the peace matters to you."[33] Her thirty "tips" for "keeping the peace" are useful starting points for grieving the death of a marriage.

For Christians the heart of the matter . . . the motives and the attitudes driving each person's behavior . . . must be shaped by Scripture. And Scripture has a great deal to say about the *heart* of the matter. Four representative verses offer guidance to Christian husbands in marital crisis:

Seek Peace

"Turn away from evil and do good; seek peace and pursue it" (Ps 34:14). The apostle Peter echoed this verse (1 Pet 3:11), then embedded it in the context of suffering *"for righteousness' sake"* (3:14). Do good to your former wife, not evil. Constantly pursue peace with her, even though she likely was the one who initiated the divorce. Do it *"for righteousness sake."* Do it so one day your children will thank you for not lashing out at their mother.

Anger Does not Produce Righteousness

"The anger of man does not produce the righteousness of God" (Jas 1:20). Anger in Scripture is rarely justified. Though we are usually quick to justify our reactions, our anger and God's righteousness are totally incompatible. Choose one or the other; you cannot have both.

Sow in Peace

"Peacemakers who sow in peace reap a harvest of righteousness" (Jas 3:18, NIV). Righteousness must remain your constant goal: only God's righteousness can clothe you for eternity. Your *"harvest"* of righteousness, the payoff or reward for pursuing and making

---

33. Covy, "Divorce without War."

peace,[34] will last forever. *Do not* allow yourself to "sow" in anger and self-pity: you really do not want that "harvest" in your life.

Suffer only for Doing Good

"If you suffer for doing good and you endure it, this is commendable before God" (1 Pet 2:20, NIV). You may believe that your divorce settlement unfairly benefitted your wife. That belief could motivate you to seek revenge at every opportunity, having determined to make her life as miserable as you possibly can. Or you could *"endure it,"* having determined to receive God's commendation on that opened-books Day of Judgment.[35] I strongly recommend the latter option.

Personal Motivations to Pursue Peace

Sir, the verses quoted above fully justify your constant pursuit of peace with your former wife. Other reasons, beyond the impact of Scripture, should also motivate you to pursue peace in your complicated, challenging relationship with her. Pursue peace for the sake of the significant people in your life, including yourself.

For the Children[36]

She will be their mother the rest of their lives. *Never* manipulate your children to gain opportunity to inflict misery on their mother. A thirst for revenge will drive your children away from you; it will destroy your credibility as a loving father and as a man of God.[37]

---

34. By definition, a peacemaker *makes* or creates peace. In both words and actions, a peacemaker deescalates and calms volatile situations.

35. Rev 20:11–14.

36. This assumes you had one or more children together.

37. A wise pastor once advised a spouse in marital distress: "Don't do anything that would cause your children to lose respect for you."

Pursuing in Pain

For the Child of God You Now Call Your "Ex"

Here I assume that she is a believer and is remaining faithful to her Lord. Scripture repeatedly suggests you should not maliciously mess with *any* fellow believer.[38] This includes your former wife. Jesus warned that you would be wiser to go swimming with a heavy stone tied around your neck than to offend her.[39] Choosing to avoid offense is ultimately far easier than treading water wearing a "millstone" life preserver!

For the Extended Families Struggling to Cope with This Rupture

Extended family members will likely struggle a great deal with your divorce. Their actions can complicate your divorce recovery; taking sides and assigning blame alienates, divides, and demoralizes. Some even become hateful, vengeful former friends. Make it hard for them to emotionally pollute your post-divorce relationship with your former wife. Pursuing peace will defuse conflict-dense and potentially dangerous family entanglements.

For Your Local Church

The church you still attend (or previously attended) will struggle less to relate to you both if you respond to her, and to them, in peace. Unless you two attend a mega-church with multiple services, one of you may need to find another local church. You will likely not be able to worship freely in the same congregation. Your primary goal must be to avoid stirring up contention among the

---

38. I suggest you find a way to bless her, even if she *feels* like an enemy. Bless her for whatever is praiseworthy: hard work, responsible care for your children, etc. Your active blessing *will* change (for the better) the quality of your future interactions. *"Do not repay . . . insult with insult. On the contrary, repay . . . with blessing"* (1 Pet 3:9, NIV).

39. *"Whoever causes one of these little ones who believe in me to sin, it would be better for him to have a great millstone fastened around his neck and to be drowned in the depth of the sea"* (Matt 18:6). I really think he meant it!

members, many of whom will grieve deeply over your divorce. *Do not* force them to "take sides" in your marital conflict.

For Yourself

You have many options for making the rest of your life miserable. In sharp contrast, you have only one option for ensuring that the rest of your life is worth living. Choose the one labeled "peace."

LISTEN TO THE LADY: PARTNERS FOR BETTER OR FOR WORSE

This chapter addressed so much it was hard for me to pin down one area to respond to. So, I decided to "go for broke" and attempt to summarize your role as a godly husband in *any* pain that affects your wife, yourself, and your marriage. *"Bear one another's burdens, and so fulfill the law of Christ"* (Gal 6:2).

There's a saying that goes: "Shared joy is a double joy; shared sorrow is half sorrow." Ecclesiastes 4:9–12[40] puts it this way:

> *"Two are better than one,*
> *because they have a good return for their labor:*
> *If either of them falls down,*
> *one can help the other up.*
> *But pity anyone who falls*
> *and has no one to help them up.*
> *Also, if two lie down together, they will keep warm.*
> *But how can one keep warm alone?*
> *Though one may be overpowered,*
> *two can defend themselves.*
> *A cord of three strands is not quickly broken."* (NIV)

---

40. Review the section titled "The *Collaborating* Principle" in chapter 2 and the TABTO principle described in the section titled "Your Longevity Advocate" in chapter 5.

Pursuing in Pain

This passage is often used to describe the advantages of a Christian marriage, with God being the third partner in the *"cord of three strands."* I believe this is true. Walking successfully through the trials you will face as a couple requires you, your wife, and the leadership of the Holy Spirit.

Pain arrives in various forms and at unexpected moments. Your wife needs you to be fully present and empathetic in each of them, regardless the cause: a financial crisis, a health crisis, the loss of a job, the loss of a child, infertility, or infidelity. The rules of engagement are the same: stay committed, keep communicating, and engage full-on in the process of healing. A painful crisis is not the time to shrink back, erect a wall, or even lick your proverbial wounds: *it's time to fight like a warrior for the one you love.*

Come "hell or high water," your wife is your partner! Partnership always demands give-and-take, cooperation, compromise, and the full commitment of both parties. Your job is not to "fix" your wife when she is sad; it's to be there to share her burden, regardless of who or what caused her grief.

If trust was broken, healing will take time, patience, and persistent participation. Never let your spouse feel like she's alone in the fight for healing and recovery. She needs your verbal, active commitment by her side, in whatever way *she* needs you to be. That may not be how you are naturally programmed, but true love is self-sacrificial.

Wounds heal only when afforded time and care. The lifetime union between a man and a woman was designed by God so that both would get the most benefit from their mates. The woman should find in marriage a shelter from life's storms and the protector of her heart. The man should find a wise helpmeet suitable for his needs. This sounds elementary, but if either of you abandon your role, you are *both* in for a rough ride.

Marriage is a beautiful journey. May you live it wide-eyed with joyful expectancy, and may you navigate any harsh terrain successfully, hand-in-hand.

DEAL WITH IT

READ AND VIEW

1. Read one or more of the following articles:

   - Bradley, "Reconciliation with a Hardened Wife."[41] This is a great article for *all* men.
   - Chinchen, "5 Ways to Pursue Your Wife."[42]
   - Edmondson, "9 Suggestions for Winning Back the Heart of Your Wife."[43]
   - Foster, "I Caught My Wife Cheating: What Now?"[44]
   - Frederick, "3 Ways I'm Pursuing My Wife & How It Multiplies Our Love."[45]
   - Gibson, "Pursuing Your Wife: Embracing a War-like Posture."[46]
   - Smalley, "Marital Infidelity: Recovery for Both Wounded Spouses."[47]
   - Colin Smith, "5 Ways to Pursue Peace."[48]

2. Attenborough, "Human Mammal, Human Hunter."[49]

---

[41]. https://familymanweb.com/2016/02/02/reconciliation-hardened-wife-reb-bradley/.

[42]. https://puredesire.org/blogs/pd/5-ways-to-pursue-your-wife.

[43]. http://ronedmondson.com/2016/11/winning-back-the-heart-of-your-wife.html.

[44]. https://www.allprodad.com/i-caught-my-wife-cheating-what-now/.

[45]. https://fiercemarriage.com/3-ways-im-pursuing-wife-multiplies-love.

[46]. https://cbmw.org/topics/leadership-2/pursuing-your-wife-embracing-a-war-like-posture/.

[47]. https://www.focusonthefamily.com/marriage/marital-infidelity-recovery-for-both-wounded-spouses/.

[48]. https://www.lifeway.com/en/articles/5-ways-to-pursue-peace.

[49]. YouTube video: https://www.youtube.com/watch?v=826HMLoiE_0.

Pursuing in Pain

THINK IT THROUGH

1. Which section of this chapter best fits your marital situation? Do you agree with its content and conclusions?
2. Was that section of the chapter the most meaningful for you? If not, which was . . . and why?
3. What marital advice could you share with a struggling married friend based on the hunter's relentless pursuit of the Eland?
4. Is pain ever a positive experience in marriage? If so, when . . . and under what conditions?

PRAY IT THROUGH

1. Pray for your wife (or former wife), asking God to give her the peace that guards her emotions and her intellect (Phil 4:7).
2. Pray for forgiveness for any feelings of anger, hatred, or longing for revenge.
3. Seek God for wisdom and endurance in your current marital situation.
4. Ask him to forgive you for things you have done or said that damaged your marriage and hurt your wife.
5. If you are still married, commit in prayer to press on (despite any pain generated by your relationship). Pray specifically for the determination to remain faithful to your marriage vows.
6. Ask God to show you ways you can:
   - Reject evil thoughts, choosing rather to *"seek peace and pursue it"* (Ps 34:14; see also 1 Pet 3:11);
   - Truly become a peace-maker who plants *"in peace"* for a future joyful harvest (Jas 3:18, NIV).

ACT ON IT

1. Identify the Scripture verse quoted in this chapter that is the most meaningful to you. Print it as a sign you can tape on your wall or mirror; alternatively, install it as the screen saver on your computer (or another device).
2. Based on the articles you have read (from the list above), list eight distinct things[50] you can do to pursue your wife or to pursue peace with your former wife. Place a new one each week in your weekly planner (paper or electronic) and use it as that week's theme or point of focus.
3. Explain to your wife (or former wife) how this chapter has impacted you.

---

50. One for each of the next eight weeks.

Bibliography

"80 Ways on How to Show Your Wife You Love Her." *Family Life Share*, June 30, 2019. https://www.familylifeshare.com/how-to-show-your-wife-you-love-her/.
Allen, Michael, and Scott R. Swain. *Sanctification*. Grand Rapids, MI: Zondervan, 2017.
Angelle, Amber. "Why Do Couples Start to Look Like Each Other?" *LiveScience*, June 26, 2010. https://www.livescience.com/8384-couples-start.html.
"Are We Happy Yet?" *Pew Research Center's Social & Demographic Trends Project*, February 13, 2006. https://www.pewsocialtrends.org/2006/02/13/are-we-happy-yet/.
Asatryan, Kira. "5 Ways to Get Your Partner to Change." *Psychology Today* (blog), April 1, 2015. https://www.psychologytoday.com/us/blog/the-art-closeness/201504/5-ways-get-your-partner-change.
Askin, Carrie. "Abusive Partners Can Change!" *Psychology Today* (blog), November 3, 2015. https://www.psychologytoday.com/us/blog/hurt-people-hurt-people/201511/abusive-partners-can-change.
Attenborough, Richard. "Human Mammal, Human Hunter." *YouTube*, November 6, 2009. https://www.youtube.com/watch?v=826HMLoiE_o.
Autenrieth, Natalia. "10 Tips on Effectively Looking for a Job While Employed." *TopResume*, September 22, 2016. https://www.topresume.com/career-advice/10-tips-on-effectively-looking-for-a-job-while-employed.
"Best Throws in NFL History." *YouTube*, January 14, 2017. https://www.youtube.com/watch?v=A_Of0jcpaKc.
Bingham, Nathan W. "What Is Sanctification?" *Ligonier Ministries* (blog), June 24, 2013. https://www.ligonier.org/blog/what-sanctification/.
Bonior, Andrea. "10 Ways to Make (and Keep) Friendships as an Adult." *Psychology Today* (blog), May 25, 2016. https://www.psychologytoday.com/us/blog/friendship-20/201605/10-ways-make-and-keep-friendships-adult.
Boyes, Alice. "9 Types of Entitlement Tendencies and How to Overcome Them." *Psychology Today* (blog), March 4, 2013. https://www.psychologytoday.com/blog/in-practice/201303/9-types-entitlement-tendencies-and-how-overcome-them.

Bibliography

Bradley, Reb. "Guidelines for Writing a Letter of Reconciliation." *Ultimate Husband*, January 3, 2018. http://www.ultimatehusband.com/letter_guidelines.htm.

———. "Reconciliation with a Hardened Wife." *The Familyman*, February 2, 2016. https://familymanweb.com/2016/02/02/reconciliation-hardened-wife-reb-bradley/.

Britec. "Easy Way to Block Adult Websites." *YouTube*, February 9, 2016. https://www.youtube.com/watch?v=wlWwEFLg20o.

"Broken Together." *YouTube*, May 20, 2014. https://www.youtu.be/RhxEL0-uD3c.

Bryan, Van. "Heraclitus: The Fire and the Flux." *Ancient Wisdom for Modern Minds*, January 22, 2014. https://classicalwisdom.com/philosophy/presocratics/heraclitus-fire-flux/.

Canfield, Ken. "What Children Gain When You Love Their Mom." *All Pro Dad*, July 18, 2014. https://www.allprodad.com/what-children-gain-when-you-love-their-mom/.

Caputo, Joseph. "Testing the Hope Diamond." *Smithsonian.com*, November, 2010. https://www.smithsonianmag.com/science-nature/testing-the-hope-diamond-63311794/.

Chapman, Gary. *The 5 Love Languages: The Secret to Love that Lasts*. Chicago: Northfield, 2015.

———. "Raising Socially Competent Kids." *Focus on the Family* (blog), October 25, 2016. https://www.focusonthefamily.com/parenting/raising-socially-competent-kids/.

Chinchen, Tyler. "5 Ways to Pursue Your Wife." *Pure Desire* (blog), February 8, 2018. https://puredesire.org/blogs/pd/5-ways-to-pursue-your-wife.

Church, Carol. "Coping with Change in Your Marriage." *SMART Couples*. https://smartcouples.ifas.ufl.edu/married/coping-with-problems-and-challenges/coping-with-change-in-your-marriage/.

Claflin, Vikki. "A Lesson for the Menfolk: How to Seduce Your Wife." *Better After 50*, May 7, 2015. https://betterafter50.com/how-to-seduce-your-wife/.

Covy, Karen. "Divorce Without War: 30 Tips for an Amicable Divorce." June 13, 2017. https://karencovy.com/divorce-without-war-30-tips-for-an-amicable-divorce/.

Crabtree, Sam. "Affirming Your Spouse." *YouTube*, June 9, 2014. https://www.youtube.com/watch?v=bfJx8N4sy6E.

"Cultivating Collaboration: Don't Be so Defensive!" *YouTube*, May 26, 2015. https://www.youtu.be/vjSTNv4gyMM.

Cummings, Michael J. "The Hound of Heaven: A Study Guide." *Cummings Study Guides*, 2011. https://www.cummingsstudyguides.net/Guides3/hound.html.

Daskal, Lolly. "The Extraordinary Power of Collaboration." *Inc.com*, April 3, 2017. https://www.inc.com/lolly-daskal/the-extraordinary-power-of-collaboration.html.

Bibliography

Dee, Jay. "Being Clean for Sex." *Uncovering Intimacy*, July 14, 2016. https://www.uncoveringintimacy.com/being-clean-for-sex/.

Desroches, Michael. "Holy Spirit: Conviction of Sin." *YouTube*, November 23, 2015. https://www.youtu.be/7njd19ya6eg.

Diller, Vivian. "Is Love Really Blind? A New Survey Provides Answers." *HuffPost*, June 12, 2012. https://www.huffpost.com/entry/physical-attraction-is-love-blind_b_1302550.

———. "Maintaining Attraction in Long-Term Relationships." *Psychology Today* (blog), May 21, 2012. https://www.psychologytoday.com/us/blog/face-it/201205/maintaining-attraction-in-long-term-relationships.

Drake, William. "How to Seduce Your Wife and Be Romantic." *BetterHelp*, April 2, 2019. https://www.betterhelp.com/advice/marriage/how-to-seduce-your-wife-and-be-romantic/.

Edmonson, Ron. "9 Suggestions for Winning Back the Heart of Your Wife." November 14, 2016. http://ronedmondson.com/2016/11/winning-back-the-heart-of-your-wife.html.

Eldred, Lisa. "5 Tips to Accountability on Smartphones." *Covenant Eyes*, April 12, 2012. https://www.covenanteyes.com/2012/04/12/5-tips-to-accountability-on-smartphones/.

Emily. "The Fact and Fiction Behind 'Two Can Live as Cheaply as One.'" *Evolving Personal Finance*, April 25, 2012. http://evolvingpf.com/2012/04/the-truth-and-fallacy-behind-two-live-as-cheaply-as-one/.

Evans, Jimmy. "Non-Sexual Affection." *YouTube*, April 18, 2012. https://www.youtu.be/XSiw_oTGgZM.

Fisher, Wyatt. "Christian Sex: Top 6 Steps to Fulfillment Within Marriage!" *ChristianCrush.com*, June 12, 2019. https://www.christiancrush.com/relationships/sexual-fulfillment-within-marriage.html.

Fonseca, Evelyn. "25 Important Bible Verses About Conviction (Shocking Verses)." *Bible Reasons*, January 23, 2019. https://biblereasons.com/conviction/.

Foster, B. J. "I Caught My Wife Cheating: What Now?" *All Pro Dad*, August 24, 2018. https://www.allprodad.com/i-caught-my-wife-cheating-what-now/.

Fottrell, Quentin. "Married Men Earn More than Everyone Else (including Married Women and Single Men)." *MarketWatch*, November 19, 2019. https://www.marketwatch.com/story/married-men-earn-more-than-single-or-married-women-and-single-men-2018-09-19.

Frederick, Ryan. "3 Ways I'm Pursuing My Wife & How It Multiplies Our Love." *Fierce Marriage*, September 12, 2016. https://fiercemarriage.com/3-ways-im-pursuing-wife-multiplies-love.

Fry, Richard. "More Americans Are Living without Partners, Especially Young Adults." *Pew Research Center*, October 11, 2017. http://www.pewresearch.org/fact-tank/2017/10/11/the-share-of-americans-living-without-a-partner-has-increased-especially-among-young-adults/.

Garbarino, Collin. "If Men Don't Want to Get Kavanaughed, They Should Follow the Pence Rule." *The Federalist*, October 3, 2018. https://

Bibliography

thefederalist.com/2018/10/03/men-dont-want-get-kavanaughed-start-following-pence-rule/.

Gibson, Greg. "Pursuing Your Wife: Embracing a War-like Posture." *CBMW*, February 27, 2014. https://cbmw.org/topics/leadership-2/pursuing-your-wife-embracing-a-war-like-posture/.

Gilbert, Marvin. *Sweaty, Sore, Sometimes Hungry: The Painful Joys of a Living Sacrifice.* Eugene, OR: Resource, 2019.

Goldman, Bruce. "Two Minds: The Cognitive Differences Between Men and Women." *Stanford Medicine*, Spring, 2017. https://stanmed.stanford.edu/2017spring/how-mens-and-womens-brains-are-different.html.

Gottman, John M. "Making Marriage Work." *YouTube*, January 30, 2018. https://www.youtube.com/watch?v=AKTyPgwfPgg.

Gottman, John M., and Nan Silver. *The Seven Principles for Making Marriage Work: A Practical Guide from the Country's Foremost Relationship Expert.* New York: Harmony, 2015.

Guillot, Craig. "The Financial Impact of Divorce." *MintLife* (blog), June 14, 2012. https://blog.mint.com/planning/the-financial-impact-of-divorce-062012/.

Heitzig, Skip. "The Four-Sided Fortress of a Husband's Love—1 Peter 3:7." *YouTube*, February 10, 2014. https://www.youtu.be/FjsHbpVzF3Q.

"The Hound of Heaven: A Modern Adaptation." *YouTube*, April 15, 2014. https://www.youtube/RXlgz4aBKt8.

"How Your Emotional Intelligence Impacts Your Professional Success, and What You Can Do About It." *CLIMB Professional Development and Training* (blog), June 30, 2017. http://climb.pcc.edu/blog/how-your-emotional-intelligence-impacts-your-professional-success-and-what-you-can-do-about-it.

"Is There Really a 7-Year Itch?" *Authentic Intimacy*, March 11, 2019. https://www.authenticintimacy.com/resources/12166/is-there-really-a-7-year-itch.

Jackson, Wayne. "What Is the Fruit of Repentance?" *Christian Courier*, 2019. https://www.christiancourier.com/articles/1015-what-is-the-fruit-of-repentance.

Jacobson, Ivy. "13 Legal Benefits of Marriage." *Theknot.com*, November 8, 2017. https://www.theknot.com/content/benefits-of-marriage.

"Johnny Lingo." *YouTube*, May 19, 2011. https://www.youtube.com/watch?v=pfahoLfrddU.

Keith, Brooke. "Growing Together in Marriage." *CBN.com*, May 7, 2015. https://www1.cbn.com/marriage/growing-together-in-marriage.

Kennedy, John F. "Ask Not What Your Country Can Do for You (Kennedy's Inaugural Address)." *UShistory.org*. https://www.ushistory.org/documents/ask-not.htm.

Klebold, Sue. *A Mother's Reckoning: Living in the Aftermath of Tragedy.* New York: Broadway, 2017.

Bibliography

Kravdal, Øystein, et al. "The Increasing Mortality Advantage of the Married: The Role Played by Education." *Demographic Research* 38 (2018) 471–512. doi:10.4054/demres.2018.38.20.

L'Abate, Luciano, et al. *Relational Competence Theory: Research and Mental Health Applications.* New York: Springer, 2010.

LaBier, Douglas. "Women Initiate Divorce Much More than Men, Here's Why." *Psychology Today* (blog), August 28, 2015. https://www.psychologytoday.com/us/blog/the-new-resilience/201508/women-initiate-divorce-much-more-men-heres-why.

Lehman, Janet. "Do Your Kids Respect You? 9 Ways to Change Their Attitude." *Empowering Parents.* https://www.empoweringparents.com/article/do-your-kids-respect-you-9-ways-to-change-their-attitude/.

Levkoff, Logan. "Fox on Sex: 5 Ways to Get Your Wife to Have More Sex with You." *Fox News*, January 14, 2015. https://www.foxnews.com/story/fox-on-sex-5-ways-to-get-your-wife-to-have-more-sex-with-you.

Loop, Erica. "How to Mend a Broken Friendship." *Oureverydaylife*, December 11, 2018. https://oureverydaylife.com/how-to-mend-a-broken-friendship-3541308.html.

Ludden, David. "How Marriage Changes Your Personality." *Psychology Today* (blog), March 15, 2018. https://www.psychologytoday.com/us/blog/talking-apes/201803/how-marriage-changes-your-personality.

Marcus and Ashley. "Growing Apart in Marriage: 7 Signs You Are Drifting from Your Spouse (and What to Do About It)." *Our Peaceful Family*, October 3, 2018. https://ourpeacefulfamily.com/growing-apart-in-marriage-signs-you-drifting-from-your-spouse-husband-wife/.

"Marriage and Men's Health." *Harvard Health*, June 5, 2019. https://www.health.harvard.edu/mens-health/marriage-and-mens-health.

"Marriage Benefits Children." *First Things First*, October 5, 2017. https://firstthings.org/marriage-benefits-children.

Mohler, Albert. "The Seduction of Pornography and the Integrity of Christian Marriage, Part 2." *The Christian Post*, June 2, 2012. https://www.christianpost.com/news/the-seduction-of-pornography-and-the-integrity-of-christian-marriage-part-2.html.

Ngu, Le, and Paul Florsheim. "The Development of Relational Competence Among Young High-Risk Fathers Across the Transition to Parenthood." *Family Process* 50, no. 2 (2011) 184–202. doi:10.1111/j.1545-5300.2011.01354.x.

Novini, Rana. "'With My Bare Hands': Alleged Killer Admits Gruesome Details." *NBC Chicago*, May 17, 2019. https://www.nbcchicago.com/news/national-international/With-My-Bare-Hands-Alleged-Serial-Killer-Admits-to-Gruesome-Murder-Details-510102591.html.

O'Connor, Gail. "What a Columbine Shooter's Mom Wants You to Know." *Parents.* https://www.parents.com/parents-magazine/parents-perspective/what-a-columbine-shooters-mom-wants-you-to-know/.

Bibliography

Oliker, Ditta. "The Importance of Fathers: Is Father's Day Real?" *Psychology Today* (blog), June 23, 2011. https://www.psychologytoday.com/us/blog/the-long-reach-childhood/201106/the-importance-fathers.

Parker, Wayne. "Key Statistics About Kids From Divorced Families." *Verywell Family*, January 7, 2020. https://www.verywellfamily.com/children-of-divorce-in-america-statistics-1270390.

Peterson, Valerie. "Here Is What You Need to Know About the Romance Fiction Genre." *The Balance Careers*, June 25, 2019. https://www.thebalancecareers.com/romance-novels-about-the-romance-fiction-genre-2799896.

Portella, Maria J., et al. "Enhanced Early Morning Salivary Cortisol in Neuroticism." *American Journal of Psychiatry* 162 (2005) 807–09. doi:10.1176/appi.ajp.162.4.807.

Powlison, David. *How Does Sanctification Work?* Wheaton, IL: Crossway, 2017.

Pruess, Angela. "Raise a Responsible Kid with These 3 Things." *Parents with Confidence*, October 26, 2017. https://parentswithconfidence.com/the-ultimate-guide-to-raising-a-responsible-kid/.

Purtill, Corinne, and Dan Kopf. "Happiness Doesn't Change Much in Long Marriages. But Something Else Does." *Quartz*, June 27, 2018. https://qz.com/1315193/how-happiness-in-marriage-changes-over-time/.

Ramirez, Vanessa Bates. "How to Stay Innovative Amid the Fastest Pace of Change in History." *Singularity Hub*, May 19, 2017. https://singularityhub.com/2017/05/19/how-to-stay-innovative-amid-the-fastest-pace-of-change-in-history/.

Ribar, David. "Children Raised within Marriage Do Better on Average. Why?" *Child and Family* (blog), Oct. 2015. https://www.childandfamilyblog.com/child-development/children-marriage-do-better-why/.

Sander, Summer. "Health Benefits of Marriage for Men & Women." *Z Living*, February 9, 2018. https://www.zliving.com/?s=Health+Benefits+of+Marriage.

Sanfilippo, Marisa. "What Is Emotional Intelligence and Why Does It Matter?" *Business News Daily*, October 24, 2019. https://www.businessnewsdaily.com/10429-emotional-intelligence-career-success.html.

Sawhill, Isabel V. "Are Children Raised with Absent Fathers Worse Off?" *Brookings*, July 15, 2014. https://www.brookings.edu/opinions/are-children-raised-with-absent-fathers-worse-off/.

Schnell, Staci Lee. "The Importance of Friendship in Marriage." *World of Psychology* (blog), July 8, 2018. https://psychcentral.com/blog/the-importance-of-friendship-in-marriage/.

Slatkin, Shlomo. "How Self-Growth Can Wreck a Marriage." *HuffPost*, January 23, 2014. https://www.huffpost.com/entry/the-enlightened-spouse-ho_b_4101313.

Smalley, Greg. "How to Pursue Your Spouse in the Long Run." *Focus on the Family* (blog), August 2, 2017. https://www.focusonthefamily.com/marriage/how-to-pursue-your-spouse-in-the-long-run/.

Bibliography

———. "Marital Infidelity: Recovery for Both Wounded Spouses." *Focus on the Family* (blog), October 22, 2015. https://www.focusonthefamily.com/marriage/marital-infidelity-recovery-for-both-wounded-spouses/.

Smith, Colin S. "5 Ways to Pursue Peace." *LifeWay*, September 14, 2017. https://www.lifeway.com/en/articles/5-ways-to-pursue-peace.

Smith, Jacquelyn. "The Dos and Don'ts of Job Searching While You're Still Employed." *Forbes*, October 26, 2012. https://www.forbes.com/sites/jacquelynsmith/2012/10/26/the-dos-and-donts-of-job-searching-while-youre-still-employed/#4bbf2da47e07.

"Social Competence." *Encyclopedia of Children's Health*. http://www.healthofchildren.com/S/Social-Competence.html.

Stanley, Scott. "Why Men Resist Marriage Even Though They Benefit the Most from It." *Institute for Family Studies* (blog), May 14, 2014. https://ifstudies.org/blog/why-men-resist-marriage-even-though-they-benefit-the-most-from-it/.

Stanton, Glenn. "Hidden Benefits of Marriage." *Focus on the Family* (blog), January 24, 2017. https://www.focusonthefamily.com/marriage/hidden-benefits-of-marriage.

———. *The Ring Makes All the Difference: The Hidden Consequences of Cohabitation and the Strong Benefits of Marriage*. Chicago: Moody, 2011.

Stibich, Mark. "How Anxiety Affects Health and Longevity." *Verywell Mind*, October 10, 2019. https://www.verywellmind.com/worry-and-anxiety-impact-longevity-2223983.

Stromberg, Lisen. "What's Love Got to Do with It? The Financial Benefits of Marriage." *Money Under 30*, November 22, 2019. https://www.moneyunder30.com/financial-benefits-of-marriage.

"Stubborn Child: Total Transformation Testimonials." *YouTube*, May 6, 2015. https://www.youtube.com/watch?v=0BCS3Q1lDjY.

Taylor, Jim. "Parenting: Respect Starts at Home." *Psychology Today* (blog), January 5, 2010. https://www.psychologytoday.com/us/blog/the-power-prime/201001/parenting-respect-starts-home.

Tenney, Tommy. *The God Chasers*. Waterville, ME: Thorndike, 2004.

Thomas, Gary. *Sacred Marriage: What If God Designed Marriage to Make Us Holy More than to Make Us Happy?* Revised ed. Grand Rapids, MI: Zondervan, 2015.

Tolpin, Angie, and Isaac Tolpin. "How to Raise Kids to Respect Their Parents." *YouTube*, January 8, 2019. https://www.youtube.com/watch?v=r41tVNIZTZU.

"Traditional 'I Do' Vows." *Wedded Your Way Officiant Services*. https://www.weddedyourway.com/traditional-i-do-vows.html.

Truitt, Janine. "Beware of the Entitlement Mentality: It Will Kill Your Progress." *HR* (blog), December 18, 2012. https://hr.toolbox.com/blogs/czarinaofhr/beware-of-the-entitlement-mentality-it-will-kill-your-progress-121912.

Verr, Ivan. "How to Seduce Your Wife Again (You Can Thank Me Later)." *Relationship Scope.com*, March 19, 2018. https://relationshipscope.com/how-to-seduce-your-wife/.

Bibliography

Waite, Linda J., and Maggie Gallagher. *The Case for Marriage: Why Married People Are Happier, Healthier, and Better off Financially.* New York: Broadway, 2001.

Walsh, Matt. "Why Religious Married Couples Are Happier." *YouTube*, May 21, 2019. https://www.youtube.com/watch?v=wOjkARou11Q.

Wehrwein, Erica A., et al. "Gender Differences in Learning Style Preferences Among Undergraduate Physiology Students." *Advances in Physiology Education* 31 (2007) 153–57. doi:10.1152/advan.00060.2006.

"What Is Respect—6 Highly Effective Ways to Teach Kids Respect." *Parenting for Brain*, December 23, 2019. https://www.parentingforbrain.com/6-controversial-tips-teaching-kids-respect/.

"What Is Servant Leadership?" *Greenleaf Center for Servant Leadership*. https://www.greenleaf.org/what-is-servant-leadership/.

"What's in It for Men? The Benefits of Getting Married." *Catholic News Agency*, March 1, 2018. https://www.catholicnewsagency.com/news/for-men-the-benefits-of-marriage-are-many-79728.

"Why Are Men Overlooking the Benefits of Marriage?" *ScienceDaily*, February 7, 2017. https://www.sciencedaily.com/releases/2017/02/170207135943.htm.

Wilcox, W. Bradford, and Nicholas H. Wolfinger. "Hey Guys, Put a Ring on It." *National Review*, February 9, 2017. https://www.nationalreview.com/2017/02/marriage-benefits-men-financial-health-sex-divorce-caveat/.

———. "Men and Marriage: Debunking the Ball and Chain Myth." *Institute for Family Studies* (blog), February 7, 2017. https://ifstudies.org/wp-content/uploads/2017/02/IFSMenandMarriageResearchBrief2.pdf.

Wilson, Chris M., and Andrew J. Oswald. "How Does Marriage Affect Physical and Psychological Health? A Survey of the Longitudinal Evidence." *SSRN*, June 3, 2005. https://papers.ssrn.com/sol3/papers.cfm?abstract_id=735205.

Zhang, Mike. "How to Seduce Your Wife: Everyday Practical Tips." *Family Life Share*, June 30, 2019. https://www.familylifeshare.com/how-to-seduce-your-wife/.

www.ingramcontent.com/pod-product-compliance
Lightning Source LLC
Chambersburg PA
CBHW051938160426
43198CB00013B/2206